C000047615

I Think It's
God Calling

Text copyright © Katy Magdalene Price 2015
The author asserts the moral right
to be identified as the author of this work

Published by
The Bible Reading Fellowship
15 The Chambers, Vineyard
Abingdon OX14 3FE
United Kingdom
Tel: +44 (0)1865 319700
Email: enquiries@brf.org.uk
Website: www.brf.org.uk
BRF is a Registered Charity

ISBN 978 1 84101 645 0
First published 2015
10 9 8 7 6 5 4 3 2 1 0

Acknowledgements
Unless otherwise stated, scripture quotations taken from The Holy Bible, New
International Version (Anglicised edition) copyright © 1979, 1984, 2011 by
Biblica. Used by permission of Hodder & Stoughton Publishers, an Hachette
UK company. All rights reserved. 'NIV' is a registered trademark of Biblica. UK
trademark number 1448790.

Scripture quotations taken from the New American Standard Bible®, Copyright
© 1960, 1962, 1963, 1968, 1971, 1972, 1973, 1975, 1977, 1995 by The Lockman
Foundation. Used by permission. (www.Lockman.org)

Cover photo: Vadym Zaitsev/Shutterstock

Every effort has been made to trace and contact copyright owners for material
used in this resource. We apologise for any inadvertent omissions or errors, and
would ask those concerned to contact us so that full acknowledgement can be
made in the future.

A catalogue record for this book is available from the British Library

Printed and bound by CPI Group (UK) Ltd, Croydon CR0 4YY

I Think It's
God Calling

A vocation diary

Katy Magdalene Price

Acknowledgements

If I can't be a good example, as someone once said, I'll just have to be a horrible warning.

This book started life as a blog, with the vague idea of helping others learn from my mistakes—although it came as a great shock to me when some people actually read it! One of those people turned out to be a commissioning editor at BRF.

The reason I wrote this book, then, is because I was asked—and also because I would have wanted to read something like this myself when I first started out on this path. I do not pretend to be a good example, or even a horrible warning. I'm certainly not 'typical' or 'representative' of the people who pursue a vocation to ordained ministry—there's no such thing. Other people's stories and perceptions will be different. What I have tried to be is honest, honest to my own personal experience and my own perception, as an 'outsider' to the church who unexpectedly found herself very much an 'insider'.

The inevitable risk of autobiographical writing is that it can appear rather self-obsessed. It's been important to me to protect the privacy of others. As a result, very few names appear in these pages, either of people or of churches. Yet none of this could have happened without them; on the contrary, other people may be the most important part of any spiritual journey. It is a personal journey, but it is not an individual one. I hope that the following acknowledgements go some way to rectifying this necessary reticence in the rest of the book.

I would like to thank all those who have supported me on this journey: the students, staff and families of the College of the Resurrection, Mirfield, and the brethren of the Community of the Resurrection; the Diocese of Manchester; the Diocese of Lincoln; the clergy and congregation of my sending church; the various churches that have welcomed me on placement; Fr Dan Sandu of Alexandru Ioan Cuza University in Iaşi, Romania; my friends and colleagues (past and present); and the Revd Naomi Starkey and her colleagues at BRF, who have done a beautiful job of making my writing publishable!

I have been fortunate enough along the way to have encountered many exceptional priests who have encouraged and inspired me. I suspect God may have realised I was a 'tricky case' and put his best people on to it! Among them are (in alphabetical order) Fr Mark Birch, Fr Paul Butler, Fr Ken Leech, the Revd Rachel Mann and the Revd Gisela Raines.

This book is dedicated, with love, to my husband Laurence and to absent friends.

Contents

Part 1

In the beginning

All I really wanted was an easy life.

I'd never quite expected to become a proper grown-up. Yet here I was in my mid-20s, having collected a degree, a job, a flat and a husband—in short, all the qualifications of respectable adulthood. For the first time since leaving home, I'd been living in the same place for more than a year. Admittedly, our north Cheshire des res was basically a garret, so small that we'd had to leave the doors off our Ikea wardrobe so we could get out of bed without injury, but the location did come with the dubious privilege of being constantly asked, 'Isn't that where the footballers' wives live?' I had caused a certain amount of consternation among my acquaintances by getting married at the radically early age of 23, and in a church at that! But it seemed to have worked out, and we were well on the slippery slope to becoming settled and productive members of society.

But something was nagging away at me. I'd started going to church. The flat was filling up with God books. Like an unrequited lover seeing their beloved's face in every crowd, I saw a dog collar in every black-jumper-and-white-top combo I spotted. Most mysteriously, I'd twice passed up the opportunity to take a law course—my supposed long-term plan—because I 'might find I want to do something else in a couple of years'.

It eventually became obvious to me, and to my husband, that my mysterious symptoms pointed to one thing: a vocation to the priesthood. There was just one problem. I didn't believe in God. My husband joked that it was a perfect qualification for the episcopate, but even he had to admit it was going to be a tough one to get past the selectors.

So, that was me off the hook.

But God can't resist a challenge. I was stubborn all right, but if there's one thing I've learned since then, it's that the God of Abraham, the God of Isaac and the God of Jacob is a whole lot stubborner. He's used to playing the long game, waiting for the moment to seize his opportunity—and when he finally did, life suddenly got interesting.

My prayer life started as an experiment.

I was a devout cradle atheist, brought up with the certain knowledge that Christianity had been disproven and that any intelligent person who still subscribed to it had merely inherited it from their parents. The irony of this was not lost on me. It was my parents' generation who had rejected God; I had never had any God to reject. The idea seemed perfectly nonsensical. Ever since a friend from an Evangelical family had told me God has a beard (we were about ten years old at the time), I'd been quite sure I knew what the word 'God' meant and it didn't relate to anything in my world.

That was a problem. Because, like the good little atheist I was, I believed in testing my own beliefs, if necessary to destruction. How could I know that my inherited atheism was sound? However barmy the idea of God appeared to me, most people clearly didn't find it meaningless at all. It was as though they knew something I didn't, and that drove me crazy.

So Christianity exasperated and enthralled me in equal measure. I had studied the history of the church for four years at university. I had studied one particular Christian— my husband Laurence—at close quarters. He had been in church choirs since he was old enough to sing, and through him I had been periodically immersed in 'high' liturgy and the Anglican choral tradition. By the age of 24 I was definitely an *Anglican* atheist, with a whole range of opinions and preferences on everything from vestments to episcopacy. The more I learned, the more beautiful it all appeared. Yet I felt no closer to understanding what was actually going on inside the heads of believers, what faith really felt like. When Laurence talked about God, the words were familiar but they might as well have been in a foreign language for all the sense they made.

The only option was to do some serious fieldwork. During my scattergun spiritual explorations, I'd picked up a varied assortment of what I supposed to be rules of the Christian life, and I did them all. Fasting, wearing a hat, saying the rosary. I went to Congregational church, Catholic church and café church. I even occasionally went along with my husband to our local parish church, until I got sick of the priest constantly asking me 'if I'd been away' (Did I look like a jetsetter? Was I particularly tanned?) but never considering that my irregular attendance might have a spiritual cause. Eventually I found a city-centre parish where they seemed unconcerned by having an atheist in the congregation and quickly signed me up to the coffee rota. It was the first time I'd regularly attended an Anglican church that didn't have my husband in the choir.

Yet still I wasn't getting the full insider experience. I needed to do something I had never done before: I needed to pray.

In retrospect, this was a ludicrously, insanely risky thing

to do. All I knew about prayer was that it involved talking to God. It had never occurred to me that God might talk back. If I'd realised I was putting myself in danger of eternal salvation, I would never have gone near it.

I didn't know how to pray but I did have a book with the word 'prayer' in the title—my grandmother's old Book of Common Prayer. I also had a Bible—because everybody has a Bible, even my parents. So, twice a day(ish) for a year, I read out the daily offices, psalms and readings, and, as I read through the history of God's saving work, I began to learn something about him. I learned that this God never chooses the obvious candidate. It was always the youngest, the weakest, the doubter and the sinner. The bigger the challenge, the more God seemed determined to overturn the odds 'for the glory of his Name'.

Within a year, it had become clear to me that my church life was the deepest, richest, truest part of my life. Even my husband thought I was pious, and he was an actual Christian. In a last-ditch attempt to rescue myself from a slide into religion, I started reading Dawkins. I even signed myself up for an Alpha course, in the hope that my stereotypes would be safely confirmed and that meeting proper scary Christians would shake me out of this religious nonsense—but to no avail. Either I had to make an absolute commitment or throw the whole thing over and accept a life lived on the surface of things.

It ought to have been a simple decision. Drift along as a non-practising atheist, with church as my kooky postmodern hobby, no strings attached, or become a Christian and instantly lose all intellectual and social credibility. Why was I even asking myself the question?

Well, that would be... the priest thing.

— ✳ —

Priesthood, it's fair to say, had never really been on the list of careers options for me. It was up there with astronaut and deep-sea fisherman as jobs that I knew existed but that were never likely to make direct contact with me. The nearest I got to considering it was a vague girlhood daydream of becoming a monk (never a nun). People ask me now, 'Why did you decide you wanted to be a priest?' The answer is that wanting had nothing to do with it.

Vocation is a malady that runs its course differently in different people. For some, the onset of symptoms is sudden and leaves no doubt about what is happening. Some people (very few) are in contexts where getting a vocation is the 'thing to do'. If you turn up to church on time and go to the odd book group, people start looking at you expectantly, wondering when it's going to develop, like the anxious parents of an adolescent with delayed puberty. Others go undiagnosed for years or even decades.

For me, it felt a bit like this: you meet someone on a train and fall in love and never see them again. You know nothing about them; you have no reason to think it would work, no evidence that the magnetic gaze of their eyes could translate into a comfortable lifelong partnership of shared coffee cups and compatible bathroom habits. Yet, in a bittersweet daydream moment, you know that the life you have is not the only one you could have had, and you wonder...

I knew nothing about priesthood. I knew that priests wore dog collars and preached sermons, and so I found myself daydreaming about wearing a dog collar and preaching a sermon. But it wasn't what I *wanted*—oh dear, no! My highest aspiration in life was to be not too conspicuously a freak. I didn't want to work with children or old people, and certainly not with religious types. I loved my free evenings and weekends. I didn't like organs and I hated hymns. Priesthood was not an ambition, a plan or even a desire; it was the last thing I wanted. Yet there it was, this *thing* I didn't yet call a vocation, an unwanted gift wrapped in golden light and the sepia glow of things that could never have been.

If I had been settled, with two kids and a mortgage and an obligation to keep my feet firmly on the ground, I might have been able to evade my vocation almost indefinitely. But instead, That Question kept coming up: 'What do you want to do with your life?' At the age of 23, having a home and a job and a husband felt like an achievement in itself—any home, any job and, frankly, any husband. By 25, people were again starting to ask me That Question, and it was getting increasingly hard to answer honestly. I couldn't say I wanted to be a priest, *obviously*, because... Well, imagine if you'd become convinced that the only route to happiness in your life was to become President of the United States. Would *you* tell anyone? But somehow all the sensible answers sounded false. It was also getting increasingly hard to hide from other people. People you'd never expect seemed to be picking up on some 'vibe'. A normally conservative Catholic priest friend stuck a biretta on my head and joked about me preaching. A jolly homeless guy who usually spoke in a succession of unintelligible bad puns broke into what sounded like prophecy. Even my mother, who had finally given up her long-cherished hope that I would become a writer (hi Mum!), tentatively suggested that I might make a career out of being 'interested in religion'.

My reasoning went like this: if someone is calling me, it has to be God. So if I am being called, there must be a God;

if there isn't, I must be going crazy. Either I'm mad or God is. Either way, I can't get on with my life until I've bottomed this one out.

What I needed was an official diagnosis. I knew that people had this thing called 'vocation', but I had no idea whether what I was experiencing was the same as what they had. What I really needed was someone to tell me, 'No, don't worry, you don't have a vocation. You're just going mad.'

Then, in April 2008, the diocese decided to hold a young persons' vocations day. I was still sufficiently new to the world of church-speak that I had to check whether I counted as a 'young person', and found that I fell into the category with a flattering few years to spare. 'All I need to do,' I figured, 'is to go along. Just to check that I have indeed taken leave of my senses and that I am absolutely 100 per cent not what they're looking for. I can sit at the back and listen and take notes—just as long as no one asks me anything about God.'

That was the rub, of course. I didn't know what a bunch of Christians would do if they caught an undercover atheist in their midst, but I was certainly going to have some awkward explaining to do

The vocations day was on Saturday, and by Tuesday I still hadn't made up my mind whether to go or not. God, it has to be said, was cutting it a bit fine. But he knew what I didn't yet know (funny how that's usually the way)—that my vocation, which was my only motivation for taking faith seriously in the first place, was also the main reason I couldn't accept faith. Truth comes with obligations; you cannot know that there is a God, know that this is the most important truth about the universe, and then just carry on as you were. Accepting God meant accepting his will for my life. I didn't want to be a priest, and as long as I didn't believe in God I had a killer excuse. If I was ever going to be a Christian laywoman, I first had to accept that it might not stop at that.

At about 11.00 in the evening, I started to say Compline, asking myself all the while, 'What would you say if someone asked, "Do you believe in God?"' At 11.30, I gave up, got up, and thought, 'Of course I do.' And I did. At 11.00 pm I didn't believe in God; at 11.30 I did, and the universe was suddenly a far more interesting place than I had ever imagined.

Help! I'm a Christian!

On the night of my conversion, I went to bed thinking it would probably wear off by morning. It didn't. By some strange providence, I was nevertheless prepared for my first day as a Christian, at least with regard to feminine accessories. I had in my jewellery case a couple of crosses: one was bought as a present for a relative whose faith inconveniently lapsed a week later, and the second I'd bought for myself but never dared wear. I put it on, feeling as if I was strapping on a sandwich-board reading, 'I was wrong—mock me' and went into work to face the music.

On the second day, I wore a bigger cross.

On the third day, I wore a rosary.

By the end of the week, I realised that nobody gave a fig. The only person to whom this was any kind of a big deal was me.

Well, I wish somebody had said it was so easy!

At school I was always one of those pretentious kids who didn't want to be pigeonholed, who wore boho chic several years before it was fashionable and listened to classic rock when everyone else was making the defining choice between Oasis and Take That. In other words, a weirdo. Now, suddenly, I had a label—'Christian'—and I was part of a tribe that includes a third of the world's population. Talk about selling out.

When it came to the young persons' vocation day, I had a pretty clear idea of the kind of person I thought would be there, and I'm afraid it wasn't flattering: an earnest teenager rocking a Jesus T-shirt, some African beads from their time digging latrines in the Gambia, and perhaps a wholly unnecessary chastity ring. I, on the other hand, had always aspired to be smart, sexy and professional—all the things the church wasn't. I might be a Christian now, but I was determined not to let it show.

So, with typical bloody-mindedness, I put on a smart skirt, a low-cut top and high-heeled boots. Of course I wanted to follow Jesus on the strait and narrow path, but I wouldn't be taking sensible shoes. Laurence was enthusiastic: 'Great!' he said. 'You look just like a woman priest!'

Great.

My plan was to slip in at the back and try not to blow my cover—and I was naïve enough about the rate of young vocations in the church to think this was a realistic plan. When I arrived, there were precisely two other 'young people' there. Nobody was talking to anybody. My cheery greeting reverberated round the room like a small nuclear explosion.

Unassuming as they were, I was intimidated by my fellow candidates. These were real, fully paid-up Christians who'd served their time in the church. Their CVs, I felt certain, would be packed with youth work, PCCs and missionary expeditions to Papua New Guinea. My only qualification for ordained ministry was looking good in black. More to the point, they actually wanted to be priests; I didn't. When the leader started by asking what we wanted to get out of the day, I raised a laugh by saying I hoped it would put me off.

But the people already in dog collars were a different matter. They seemed, to my surprise, not at all unworldly, more like someone I could imagine myself becoming. One of the group, a grinning purple-haired woman whom I instantly dubbed Rock-chick Vic, put on a video montage, illustrating vocation by means of clips from Monty Python, *The Matrix* and a whole succession of romantic clinches. I glanced about nervously. Was this a test? Should I be shocked and avert my gaze? Apparently not.

Nor were they fazed by my unusual story. After all, they had spent a lot more time around God than I had, and I was presumably no more implausible than a King David or a Zacchaeus. In fact, one thing they kept saying was, 'God doesn't choose the equipped; he equips the chosen.'

At the end of the morning session, I took my life in my hands and approached the DDO—the Diocesan Director of Ordinands. Up until this point, all I knew about the selection process for ordained ministry was that it was as long, opaque and intrusive as that for the secret services. (Actually, I can tell you, it's worse. There aren't many jobs you can do with a history degree and I've applied for most of them.) I was half expecting them to take a sample of hair and test it for drug use and heresy. I had heard tell of the DDO, God's second-in-command in matters vocational, and I'd assumed that I would have to spend months or years petitioning this lord chamberlain to grace me with an audience. Yet here he was. I did not have to go past armed guards or submit my request in triplicate or use a secret handshake. He was not sitting on a throne waiting for me to prostrate myself. He was by the buffet table, eating quiche.

I gave it to him straight: 'I'm not even baptised yet. How long is this going to take?'

'Anything from six months to two years,' he said.

'Six months to two years before I start the process, right?' I clarified.

'No, six months to two years before selection.'

And so he sent me off with my bag full of vocations literature and my head full of crazy dreams, walking on air.

The leaflets in my bag were like contraband. It felt daring and risky just to have in my possession something with the words 'vocation' and 'priest' on, words which could be hidden in the back of a drawer and taken out for my own secret pleasure. It was the beginning of a new and delicious addiction—thinking about vocation, reading about vocation, talking about vocation. Everything except actually doing something about it.

After all, I had other things to deal with. Namely, the sudden and unexpected presence of God in my life.

I had no idea how to be a Christian. I didn't know any Christians, apart from my husband—who was probably an unrepresentative example, and a bad one at that—and people from church. What did Christians do the rest of the time? What did they eat, what did they wear, where did they work? Of course, once I became a Christian I started to find out there were loads of us, and some of them even worked in the same office as I did. But wasn't there more to it than that? Weren't we supposed to give up everything we owned and... sell it to the poor, or something?

You see, I'd thought I was doing pretty well at this religion lark, right up to the point where I actually started believing in God. I went to church, said my morning and evening office, and fasted during Lent. I'd given up Primark and stocked up on Fairtrade. I seemed at least to be keeping up with the Joneses, faith-wise. But you can't have a great relationship by writing an email every day and never bothering to open the ones the other person sends back. Now suddenly I was aware of God, of God's enormous holiness and my own deficit of holiness, and of the infinite distance that placed between us. If the idea of an atheist priest was ridiculous, I seemed an even less plausible candidate now. Before I could presume to be of any help to anyone else, I needed to 'get enlightened', preferably as quickly as possible.

My first problem was that I didn't speak Christian. A religion is as much a culture as a set of beliefs, and I found myself a hapless ex-pat in my new foreign home. My attempts to fit in misfired desperately. Why had I thought all Christians were pro-Palestinian? Where had I got the idea that Christianity was opposed to cremation? Why did nobody warn me about expressing an innocent penchant for dark wooden pews and eastward-facing Communion services?

Money was a minefield of euphemisms. Non-refundable deposits suddenly became 'offerings'; 'stewardship' could mean anything from environmental concerns to Gift Aid and standing orders. Prayer was even worse. The same word, 'prayer', seemed to refer to talking and to being silent, to mental images and to absence of images—in fact to almost anything. On retreat I was constantly being asked, 'Where was God in that?' or 'What is God doing in your life?' Once I was advised to 'arrange to meet Jesus and go on a walk together'. Something was getting lost in translation.

When I first approached the church asking for a spiritual director, it was as a confused atheist looking for, well, some kind of direction in matters spiritual. One diocese kindly but redundantly explained the parish system to me; another ignored my email entirely. When I did finally obtain a diocesan list of those offering spiritual direction in my area, it was from the Diocesan Director of Ordinands. I can't help thinking it says more than it should about the church's true attitude towards lay people, if the only members of the laity who are assumed to need spiritual directors are potential clergy.

The list was an unintentional comic masterpiece. A paraphrase might be, 'Here is a list of spiritual directors, although directors isn't really the best word for it. They aren't necessarily any better than any others who aren't on the list. They simply have more experience. Not that experience is necessarily a good thing, of course.'

This strange coyness about the ministry they offered also afflicted many of those on the list. If the same approach were extended to the Yellow Pages, it might read like this: 'Plumber. I am 45 years old, blessed with a lovely wife, Ruth, and for the last ten years I have been really enjoying accompanying people in exploring their drainage systems.' But my favourite line has to be the following: 'By its very nature, this list is public, but we recognise the essential hiddenness of this ministry.' If I was looking for someone to translate Christianese, these people were certainly fluent speakers!

At this point my cultural atheism kicked in. Approaching the choice with the same logic as I would use when picking out a washing machine, I wrote up a shortlist. Then I contacted them all to try-before-you-buy. As social faux pas go, this is up there with the time I booked three blind dates back-to-back in one evening: it gets some funny looks but it's undeniably efficient. However, I suspect there was a bit of behind-the-scenes input from the Spirit. Out of 46 people, the one I was led to was the purple-haired priest from the vocations day.

I'd imagined that I was about to put myself under the discipline of some sage or guru who would hold me accountable for my obedience to a strict rule of life. Instead, I was invited to have a cup of tea every couple of months and work on 'feeling lovable'. With her help I gradually (*very* gradually) learned to 'let go' and bask in God's presence. I was not a good student. I wanted to know what prayer was *for*, and how you knew when you were doing it, and, most of all, how to do it *right*. Like a long-suffering driving instructor with a nervous pupil, God had to spend ages encouraging me to release my petrified grasp on the controls for long enough to be able to go anywhere.

All this time, my vocation remained in the back of the drawer. I had fallen head-over-heels in love with God, and, like a would-be bride expecting a long engagement, I was enjoying the novelty of being a lay Christian. I was in no hurry to give it up. In fact, I was rather resentful of God for still going on about vocation. However little I knew about priesthood, I knew this: priests are busy people. Not for them the stable routine which (all the authorities say) is so essential to a healthy prayer life. If I was going to do a first-class job of being a priest, did that mean settling for being a second-class Christian?

Shortly after my baptism, I went on pilgrimage to Taizé in France. As I was kneeling alone at the front of a tiny village church, the seats behind me started to fill up. I felt uncomfortable at being so conspicuous, and it occurred to me: if I become a priest, it will be like this all the time. Of course, I had started to learn that all Christians are public Christians; even at work I was sometimes called upon to defend 'religion', which seemed to mean a strange amalgam of Islam, medieval Catholicism and American fundamentalism. I even enjoyed that public ministry and the realisation that people around me had so many spiritual questions they'd been waiting to ask. But my new faith was still fragile and I was sometimes shocked at how thin-skinned I'd become.

Why was I always the one who got herself *involved*? Why did I have to stick my head above the parapet? I obviously didn't know the first thing about the spiritual life, so, just this once, couldn't I be the one sitting at the back minding her own business?

All of this sounded very sensible and patient and humble. With due patience, humility and prudent caution, then, I told God he'd got it wrong.

So why did I still feel as if something more was being asked of me? I went through every possibility. I spent a fortnight contemplating voluntary poverty. I thought I discerned a call to celibacy (which would have been slightly inconvenient for my husband!) for about a week. Finally I got to the bottom of the list, and priesthood was still there.

God wanted me to give something up all right—my pride; my freedom to tell him that it was my life and I had a better idea, thank you very much. You can't point at somebody else's path and say, 'That one looks good. I'll have the same as her, thanks.' If you follow, you have to go where he leads... in my case, a coffee shop in Manchester.

Testing times

Let us pause for a moment for a brief excursus on 'The Process'. The Process is that remarkable alchemical method by which candidates are sifted and refined and shiny new potential priests are magically extracted. It goes like this.

You start with your parish priest, who will send you to the Diocesan Director of Ordinands (DDO), who may send you to one of his Assistants (ADDOs), who will send you to two Vocations Advisers (VAs), who will send a report to the DDO, who will send you to the Examining Chaplain, who will send a report to the DDO, who will send a report to the bishop, who will send you to the BAP (the Bishop's Advisory Panel, not a bread roll to have with your alphabet soup). The DDO will send a report to the BAP, which will send a report to the bishop, who will then send you to college. Or not, as the case may be.

It's OK, we'll go over this more slowly later on. Much more slowly.

Before you can go anywhere, though, you need to talk to your parish priest. To the church, it seems obvious that your parish priest will be the person who knows you best and can best advise you. To anyone more used to the secular world, it's a bit like going to your GP to ask about doing a medical degree. In my case, the new rector had been in post all of one month when I had my close encounter with God, and it seemed a bit harsh to land the poor chap with an enquiry about baptism, confirmation and ordination all in one go. It was also just downright cheeky. How could I, barely through the doors of the church, tell the incumbent I thought I could do his job? So it was with something approaching abject terror, several months after my baptism, that I called the rector and made my date with destiny in a coffee shop in central Manchester.

The whole meeting was farcical. I had prepared a form of words which I hoped would ease us gently into the conversation. I would steer clear of the heavy stuff—like priesthood, vocation or God. I was 'interested in exploring ordained ministry'. The phrase sounded modest and on-message, and I was very pleased with it. In the event, I almost had to go for my train without ever having broached the subject. It was 45 minutes before I got the rector's attention away from his conversation with the café manager, and another five before I managed to wrest the conversation off the tangent that my 'subtle' approach had inadvertently set it on. When the rector finally got the message, I'd like to say he was delighted, or surprised, or even horrified—but the best description would be 'cautious'. In fact, he used the word 'cautious' several times. Diplomatically, he avoided expressing any opinion on my vocation or asking me any questions about it. Instead, he warned me that nobody should become a priest unless they absolutely had to. He recounted anecdotes about the devastation that priesthood can wreak on one's home life. He spoke positively about the superiority of non-stipendiary (unpaid) ministry. By the time he'd finished, I almost feared he might have talked himself into resigning.

Finally, he sent me away with two pieces of homework—to read a couple of relevant books... and to pray for my vocation to go away. The DDO had been very clear that the discernment process should get moving as soon as possible, but getting things moving, apparently, meant putting them on hold.

Over the next few months, I became familiar with a new piece of Christian vocabulary: 'test'. According to all the vocations literature, what one should do with a vocation is to test it. I wasn't sure what this meant, but I imagined it must be something like the Temptation in the Wilderness. After fruitless hours of internet searching, it turned out that the elusive but essential 'testing' meant nothing more than reading, praying, talking to people... and, most of all, waiting.

One of the main ways to test a vocation, I learned, is to ignore it. Give it time. Push it away. True vocations, it seems, are plants that flourish with neglect. Not for the C of E the divine impatience of a St Paul or the passionate urgency of the prophets. This is England, where queuing is an endurance sport. I needed to hurry up and wait.

That meant a pretty major reassessment of my life. My mid-20s, I had always assumed, would be times of change and movement and growth. All around me, my friends and contemporaries were doing new things—weddings, babies, houses. They were moving to London or moving out of London, moving jobs or losing jobs, getting ahead or getting out, upscaling or downsizing.

For me, all of that was ruled out for the foreseeable future. Unofficially, I'd heard that I needed to be in the same parish for at least two years. Worse, I'd heard stories of newlyweds and new parents being punished with a time penalty of two to five years for daring to make an unauthorised major life change.

For me and Laurence, that meant some very serious questions. It meant Laurence putting on hold his own career plans. It also meant facing up to my biological clock. Five years earlier, when I couldn't imagine ever being as old as 30, we'd agreed to start a family by the start of my fourth decade. Now pregnancy was breaking out across the office where I worked, and I was crazy on second-hand hormones. Doing the mental arithmetic, if selection took two years, and training three, and female fertility declines by 3.5 per cent per year after the age of 30... The dilemma could only be solved in one way: if I was going to do this, it had to be in the next three years. I craved the freedom to explore my spiritual life, to try things out, to take my time. But I couldn't build my life—our life—around something that might never happen.

Testing might not involve quite so many demons as I'd imagined, but that didn't mean it was easy. Sometimes it seemed as if I couldn't open my mouth without saying something that proved I didn't have a true vocation. I told one priest that it was ordained ministry to which I felt called, not licensed lay ministry. She advised me to be more open and not jump to conclusions. So on my next conversation with a member of the clergy, I expressed my openness to all the options—only to be told that people with true vocations know for certain. As a layperson in the pews, I had been blissfully ignorant of the angst-filled debates over the meaning and future of ministry. Never describe priesthood as a job or (worse still) profession: God forbid that professional standards like excellence, fairness or transparency should taint the venerable institution of priesthood. But don't, for goodness' sake, wax lyrical about being set apart for the sacred ministry of the altar; that's a clear sign you're only in it for the power and the lace. Best of all, just don't have a vocation at all, since thinking you have one is probably proof that you don't.

I started to think the clergy were all in on it, that this was some secret church policy for testing candidates' dedication, possibly borrowed from the practice of Eastern gurus in films. Most of the time, I felt hopelessly out of tune with the church and hopelessly out of my depth. I signed up to a diocesan course on ministry, which gave me the precious comradeship of others on the same journey. Yet, in the first session, I was left looking like the class dunce because I didn't know the verse reference for my favourite biblical passage. (Has everyone else in the class *memorised the entire Bible*?) Another time, I managed to derail a whole lecture on intercessory prayer with one innocent question.

There were times when I desperately wanted someone who was just straightforwardly on my side, someone to whom I could moan about the whole situation. But if there's one thing that's taken as cast-iron proof that your vocation isn't genuine, it's any questioning or complaining about the discernment process. Once you start, you are expected to show complete deference to The Process. I was trapped in a paradox: I had to believe God was really calling me, but I also had to accept that the wider church might tell me he wasn't. But if they said 'no', what did that mean for my faith? I knew God only as the God who calls, the God who had called me. If I was wrong about this, what if I was wrong about the whole God thing?

But there were moments, moments when God seemed to catch my eye across a crowded room and give me a secret look that said, 'We're in this together.' One of those moments came right at the beginning, just after I'd met with the rector. It was a dark and stormy night, and I was standing on a railway platform when it occurred to me: what *is* priesthood, anyway?

I had no idea!

I was horrorstruck. I had been pursuing this sense of calling, yet I had never once thought to ask *what* I was called to, apart from the empty word 'priesthood'. Suddenly, on the rainy platform, I had one of those moments of feeling 'rapt up' to the heavens, energised by the Spirit. A priest, I thought, is like the bread of the altar—in itself an empty vessel, worthless, nothing; by the grace of God, everything. When I came home, I opened the book the rector had lent me: *The Christian Priest Today* by the former Archbishop Michael Ramsey. There it was in the first chapter: 'You are Everything and Nothing, o Priest.'

My 'testing' for the last year had consisted mostly of reading books and getting acclimatised to the Church of England. I had been introduced to the ways of PCCs, inducted into the mysteriously named role of 'sidesman' and shown the drill of serving at the liturgy. At one point I even found myself on the children's team, my protestations that I'd never worked with children in my life (and even, in desperation, that I didn't like children anyway) apparently unable to overcome the indisputable fact of my being female. Most important of all was washing up. Forget preaching, leadership and pastoral sensitivity; I was advised that washing up was the task on which every priest was judged, and that, should I be ordained, I should seek out every opportunity to justify my stipend by the conspicuous use of rubber gloves and Fairy Liquid.

The next step was a placement in a different parish. I was deeply impressed by the priest I was assigned to shadow. She didn't seem to spend her time anguishing about the dilemmas that filled so many pages of the books now lining my walls. She just did what was in front of her. From pastoral care to child care, from chairing a meeting to varnishing a pew, she met the needs of the congregation as they presented themselves. And yes, she did the washing up—automatically and without fanfare, like anyone else. She had a sufficiently strong sense of her own diaconal and priestly vocation that her ministry was not diminished by the many things she did which were not explicitly priestly. On the contrary, by doing them as a priest, it seemed that she incorporated and sanctified them as part of her ministry. I admired her... and stood absolutely no chance of successfully imitating her, though she was kind enough to disagree. How did she find the energy to do half a dozen jobs for which she'd never been trained, while subsisting on a diet of cup-a-soups and crackers? More to the point, was an organisation which expected that of her really one I wanted to work for? But it was soon made clear that this, too, was one of those doubts it was better not to voice.

And so I was ready to see the DDO.

What?

You mean... we're still right at the beginning?

'Fraid so.

Nearly two years after our first buffet-side encounter, I was finally going to visit the DDO formally and be dropped into the top hopper of The Process. I arrived at the diocesan offices, where the DDO's secretary said she would 'put me in the chapel'. Supposing (wrongly) that such an exalted person-age as the DDO would certainly have his own private office, I assumed I had been sent there to spiritually 'freshen up', and made a futile attempt to pray and touch up my make-up at the same time, while I waited to be called. When the door opened, therefore, I was kneeling on the floor, rummaging in my handbag.

The DDO looked down at me kneeling at his feet in the chapel. 'Oh, very pious,' he said.

When I had recovered my composure and the contents of my handbag, he explained my next step: fill in a form. It was described as a 'vocation enquiry' form and asked basic questions such as where I went to church and how long I'd been considering ordained ministry. It included a criminal records check, which seemed somewhat overcautious, since the only person it authorised me to work with was the DDO.

I checked, was that everything? Yes, it was confirmed, I had indeed waited weeks for an appointment and taken a day off work, a train and a bus, to pick up a form.

But from then on, things went remarkably smoothly. Not quickly, of course—this is the church, after all, a national organisation with the ethos of a village fête committee, where there's never any rush and it's always easier to 'just pop round' than to send an email. In fact, I never did work out whether all the breathing space in the timetable was the result of principle or inefficiency. The only thing I was told about my two interviews was that I must leave at least three weeks between them. I had, and still have, no idea what difference three weeks is supposed to make. But if it wasn't quick, it was easy—maybe too easy.

Having prepared for a tough interview, I was taken off my guard by the Anglican technique of tea and a chat. In fact, so well prepared was I that I didn't want to leave until I had spouted out everything I wanted to say in answer to the questions I thought they should have asked me. The resulting report was as pleasant and easy-drinking as the beverage: we assume everything is fine; some things didn't come up; and she does talk a lot, doesn't she?

Until this point, I had been afraid that I wouldn't get through. Now I was afraid that I would. A few more cups of tea and a little less conversation, and I could be out in a parish without a clue.

From this point on, a new phrase entered my daily conversation: 'If all goes to plan...'. I still didn't feel bold enough to admit that my going to theological college was a real possibility, but Laurence and I had to plan our lives around it nevertheless, and so the euphemism was born.

Over time (perhaps, loath as I was to admit it, by that same mystical activity of waiting that seemed to play such a large part in The Process), my vocation had become less defensive and more peaceful. It was no longer unrequited love. Nor was it at that jagged and touchy rollercoaster stage of a new relationship, all neurotic texts and slammed doors and tearful reconciliations. It was reaching that comfortable phase where it and I cohabited complacently, and marriage was simply a reality that hadn't yet been spoken of.

During this time, I got a promotion at work, to a far more stimulating job, leading a training project. That resolved another question which had been nagging away at me from the beginning: was all this just my way of finding something to do with my life? Was it merely a craving for new beginnings, an interesting diversion from my happy but uneventful life? In my new job I was constantly busy, stimulated, creative—and, sure enough, my vocation went away... for one week. My new job didn't fill the gap. It just confirmed that I loved teaching adults and I loved managing projects and I got a buzz from tight deadlines and juggling priorities—all of which seemed to fit rather well with what God might be calling me to.

Three years before, all I'd wanted was an easy life. I didn't like being conspicuous and I didn't like getting up to speak in front of people, and I certainly didn't like stress. God doesn't choose the equipped. He equips the chosen.

Reality check

The final, national stage of The Process is the BAP, the three-day Bishop's Advisory Panel, formerly known as the Selection Conference, formerly known as a whole series of other acronyms (the changes provide a useful alternative to carbon-dating for priests). Now, the chats and quiche would give way to more corporate language of 'criteria' and 'potential'. The BAP was my chance to have my vocation validated by the wider church. It was also the point at which I could really, absolutely and terminally, fail. Until then, it had all been about 'readiness', but at BAP, I would only get two chances. At the time, it was two strikes and you were out—for life.

Now there was only one man standing between me and BAP: the Examining Chaplain. The name sounded, not inaccurately, like some kind of low-ranking inquisitor. But first I needed to fill in The Form. Oh yes. This is the Form of Forms, before which the American Tax Return quails and the Enhanced DBS falls silent.

One way in which selection for ordained ministry differs from secular recruitment is that God can call people of all ages, professions and educational backgrounds. Fisherman, tax official or accessory to murder; there is no standard set of appropriate qualifications and experience. Assessment of candidates therefore has to be carried out in what might be considered a fairer way, looking directly at personal qualities.

The downside of this is that everything in your life is potentially relevant. In secular recruitment it is generally considered bad form, if not downright illegal, to ask about a person's private relationships, sex life, traumatic childhood and personal faith. In the church, the opposite is the case. I was asked to give my life story—and that was just one question. After years of selling myself in job applications, ticking the boxes and learning the right corporate clichés, there was something rather wonderfully subversive about a system that encouraged honesty. At last I had the chance to give God the glory for leading me out of depression, for sending me my husband, for giving me the confidence and faith to be ten times the person I had ever been without him.

At the same time, it was horrifically intrusive. I was being asked to make myself as vulnerable as I would to a spiritual director or confessor, but with a crucial difference: these people *were* there to judge me. No more 'feeling lovable'. They were strip-searching my soul, and maybe my faith and my personality would be found not good enough for God.

With the form safely written and sent, all ten pages of it, I took myself off to glorious Bath for a friend's hen party. At some stage after the treasure hunt but before I got up on the table for 'Dancing Queen', my phone rang. It was the Examining Chaplain. I did my best impression of a sober and plausible future clergywoman, trying to wipe from my mind the pink devil horns on my head and the sight of my friend importuning innocent passers-by with phallic drinking straws. 'Yes,' I said, 'that date will be absolutely fine. Thank you so much for calling.'

The time for tea and chats was past. The Examining

Chaplain was a fellow Oxbridge history grad and we set to it hammer and tongs like a third-year tutorial. There was a pretty sticky moment when he accused me of being opposed to infant baptism—presumably because I had neglected to get myself baptised as a baby—and I didn't really know how to rectify that, short of inventing time travel. But it must have gone all right, because several weeks later (when I next managed to get an appointment with the DDO, since anything this urgent couldn't possibly be emailed) I was given the news: I was good to go.

So the date was set. I was to go to BAP in May, which gave me as much time as possible to prepare. Nine months, in fact.

Since it was clearly far too early to start preparing in earnest, I allowed myself only the briefest indulgence in BAP obsession. On the grounds that 50 per cent of organisation is having the right stationery, I prepared a new pink ringbinder, a bright fresh set of file dividers and a detailed preparation schedule for the months January to May. Then I put it away and refused to look at it until the new year.

But by January I was a wreck.

In October, Laurence's job had turned into an 'efficiency saving' and he took a temporary job, working twelve-hour night shifts in a bank's Complaints department. In the mornings, I would get up quickly, grab my clothes and scoot out of the room so that he could fall into bed without a word. At night, I would come home to an empty drive, an empty house and a shapeless, endless evening. Our routine—and our relationship—was on hold.

He lost track of days. I lost track of months. Our summer holidays, delayed from August to September to October as we both waited for news about our jobs, were then indefinitely postponed until they slipped off the end of the calendar entirely. Christmas came and went while I was still mentally around mid-November; I turned 28 without warning. When January arrived, it joined the backlog of months awaiting my attention, and the pink folder remained in its place.

Worst of all was the effect on my prayer life. Silence is like a vacuum: it gets filled. Three years before, I had made space in my life and had been astounded to find it suddenly filled with God. This time, what filled my solitude was just a flotsam and jetsam of obsessive thoughts, irrelevant memories and emotional non sequiturs, the waste products of my life playing behind my eyes like my own personal out-takes video.

It happened almost imperceptibly. There had always been occasions when I missed or abbreviated my prayers, without ceasing to think of myself as someone who prayed twice a day. I didn't stop thinking about prayer or wanting to pray. It became so easy to substitute the intention for the act that it was a while before I noticed I wasn't doing it any more. I had stopped praying.

So this is the dark night of the soul—and the demons that inhabit it are not, after all, the old favourites of lust and greed and anger, but the white noise of life.

It did occur to me that this was the sort of scenario in which people might seek help from the church, but my relationship with the church had also changed. At some point, I had crossed an invisible line—from being one of the people 'out there' for whom the church exists to being one of the people 'in here' who exist (it felt to me) for the church. I was no longer a consumer but a human resource. Without having any kind of official leadership role, I had nevertheless begun to experience the isolation familiar to those who exercise public ministry.

What did it was the references. I had been told early on that I would be needing two references from my church, one from the priest and one from a lay member. From that moment, I suddenly had something to prove. I was constantly expecting someone to rebuke me with the words, 'And you think you're going to be a priest?'—although, of course, nobody ever did. I felt acutely the truth that 'no prophet is without honour except in his own town'. How could I ever look like a potential ordinand to people who had known me as an atheist, hacking my way through the unfamiliar hymns just a few years before? The church was no longer a place to encounter God but an arena in which to prove myself, to play the role of robust and reliable rota-fodder. So much for 'My power is made perfect in weakness.'

If I'd been concentrating more on my Bible reading, I might have remembered something important. Whenever you're in a tight spot, God's always there before you. He sent Joseph to prepare the way for the starving Israelites and placed Esther in the palace in preparation for the day her people would need her intercession. If life were an action movie, God would be the one who builds the hatches into the top of lifts, and the conveniently large service tunnels.

In this case, the escape hatch was a train—a train I'd booked months earlier, in completely different circumstances, and had simply been too lethargic to cancel. It was waiting for me on the platform at the end of January, to whisk me away for a week in Devon to spend some quality time with God.

I arrived backwards, up a 1-in-4 ascent, jammed into my taxi seat by five other people plus baggage. This was genuine Lorna Doone country, this curve of pasture with the cliffs falling into the sea before it and the wild red heath of the valley at its back. Here a bandit lord could hold out indefinitely against the law, and a runaway ordination candidate against the noonday demons.

For the first time in a long while, I spent some time in godly leisure pursuits, the hidden things which weren't going to earn me any CV points but which got God back into my system—walking, painting, writing poetry, and, most of all, just sitting on the rocks by the beach and letting the round sea rub smooth the pebble of my soul. In all this time that I'd been seeking to do God's will, somehow God himself had got lost from sight, crowded out by The Process.

The text I kept coming back to over those days was about Mary of Bethany, pouring out costly perfume out of pure exuberant love for her Lord. She was accused of being useless, of getting above her station, of drawing attention to herself. Yet all she wanted to do was to point attention towards him, to glorify God with the 'useless' superfluity of worship. And so I was brought back to the place where I started: 'everything and nothing', the empty vessel, waiting to be filled by the grace of God and poured out for his glory.

Over the next few months, back home, I realised something else: it was OK if they said no. God wasn't going to go away. A 'no' from the church didn't mean my relationship with God was all in my head.

To prepare myself for the possibility of disappointment, I began to make a list of consolation prizes for if things did not, in fact, 'all go to plan'. I promised myself everything I'd wanted to do and never had the time or courage for. I would learn the cello. I would get fit. I would take out my vintage sewing machine and sign up for evening classes in dressmaking. Maybe I would even write that book, and make my mother proud. Best of all, I would dye my hair pink—sugar candy pink, in a 1920s bob.

Suddenly, failure was starting to sound like a plan!

This was my very own Last Temptation, in pocket-size edition. I had been fighting for three years for the right to give up my freedom. Here, on the very threshold, I was suddenly aware of all the other crazy dreams I could be pursuing, none of which now seemed all that crazy in comparison.

The most tempting prospect of being rejected, though, was simply getting back to being a proper layperson—having the focus of my spirituality on prayer and daily life rather than being busy in church. For the last three years, my life had felt provisional. I had tried and failed to find God in my daily life and work, to live in the present rather than the future. If I got given the 'all clear'—no vocation to priesthood—then at least my life would be able to continue. I would have the right to be a layperson, to say to God, 'I tried; you can't ask any more.'

The only answer I feared was 'maybe'—that the church, to whom I was still a 'young person' with all the time in the world, would ask me to 'give it a bit more time'. But three years of waiting and hoping and jumping through hoops had trashed my spiritual life. It had distorted my relationship with the church, turned pastors into judges and prayer into an assessment.

I was going to give it one shot. Then, either way, yes or no, there was such a thing as a future again. At last, the brakes were coming off my life.

Being myself

I prepared for BAP mostly by cooking. It was Lent, the perfect time for home-cooked veggie curries, and there is something holy-wholesome about the rhythms of chopping onions and grinding spices.

I also had to start facing up to the possibility that it might really be happening. Until then, I'd been reluctant to tell too many people about my plans. I didn't want to set myself up for embarrassment if I fell at the first hurdle. It was only once I had a date for BAP that I felt it was no longer just my crazy and presumptuous idea but a realistic prospect in the eyes of people who ought to know.

Having heard the tales of other people in my situation, I'd steeled myself for possible hostility and a lot of awkwardness from my less religious friends, as if I were announcing that I was giving up drink, sex and swearing, and getting a complete personality transplant. In the event, the most common response I got was 'Do you want to be a bishop?' closely followed by 'Aren't priests Catholic?' and other variations on the priest/vicar confusion. I quickly developed a potted explanation of this distinction, by analogy with GPs and doctors. The reply coming in at unexpected third place was 'My sister does that.' Apparently my plans were not so uniquely eccentric after all; priesthood could crop up even in the most normal families.

As for churchgoing friends, they couldn't have been more supportive. I was more afraid of letting them down. Quite a number reassured me, 'If you've got this far, you're bound to get through', a sentiment that would have been encouraging had it not been patently false. Even friends who were opposed to female ordination took it in their stride. My fears about 'coming out' as an ordination candidate had been entirely unfounded, and I only wished I'd shared my plans with my friends and sought their support much sooner.

As for my family, I don't know why I worried. My mother, after all, was the one who reacted to my engagement three months before my finals with an indifferent 'Oh. You'd better tell your dad.' As it happened, I didn't need to tell them at all. It was my sister who told *me*, 'Mum and Dad said you're in training for the ministry.' I'd been concentrating so hard on not letting it slip that it took a few nonplussed moments before I realised it was her and not me who had brought it up. 'Erm... they haven't quite got that right.'

'So you're not planning to be a vicar, then?'

'Well, yeah, probably. But anyway...'

The most difficult conversation was the one I hadn't expected at all—with Laurence. My husband had always been the one who believed in me unconditionally. He was less prepared for my failure than I was. Although he'd always accepted my vocation as mine (he'd never tried to muscle in on the act with talk of 'our' vocation, like the men who say 'We're pregnant' even though they aren't the ones vomiting every time they smell cheese or coffee), he'd always known it was something we were doing together, something that would mean a change in both our lives. So I was taken aback when it came out: he felt *stuck*. Stuck here because of The Process, and then, if things 'went to plan', looking forward to being stuck at college for three years and stuck in my curacy for the next three. 'When does it stop?' he asked. 'When is it not just me following you round the country?' I was horrified. I could only repeat my promise that if I didn't get through, it would be his turn to pursue his dreams. He finished by saying, 'I know you believe in service and sacrifice' and didn't mention it again. But I wasn't going to forget that. Service and sacrifice—my service but his sacrifice.

I had practical things to attend to, as well—collecting my references and explaining to my referees that, yes indeed, they were required to comment on my personal faith and family life. It was amusing to see the culture clash as the ethos of the church was brought forcibly together with that of my workplace. Take the church's latest buzzword, 'leadership'. It's an impressive word, and my manager agreed: in five years of work, I had done nothing impressive enough to count as leadership. But as far as the church was concerned, I'd collected an excellent portfolio of leadership positions: I'd even been on the committee of the university History Society!

It was only when reading what others saw in me that I slowly recognised: yes, that is me. It was humbling to read that I was 'effective' and 'resilient' and 'took criticism cheerfully'. That was the first I'd heard of it! I was like a mother who still checks with her student son if he needs to go to the loo before they go out. I had got so used to thinking of myself as a hapless overgrown adolescent, I hadn't stopped to notice everything that God had been doing in me.

But one reference was still outstanding. The rector had been playing his cards close to his chest from the beginning and I still didn't know if I had his support. The deadline came and went and still no news.

So... that was it, then. No BAP.

Why haven't I heard from the DDO? Why is nobody else freaking out about this?

Of course, I should have known. 'Deadline' is another word that has its own special definition in the C of E. I got through to the DDO's secretary. 'Oh, don't worry,' she said. 'They're used to us.'

Some people will tell you that BAP is impossible to prepare for and impossible to manipulate. They advocate a policy of saying the first thing that comes into your head, on the premise that spontaneity is a sign of sincerity—a theory which has been responsible for some pretty dire liturgy and some worse love poetry. Others drill themselves in everything that could possibly come up and use every strategy to give themselves an edge. I was even offered under-the-counter documents from someone's DDO (I turned them down). Common advice was to 'be myself', which is wise counsel indeed as the aim of a lifetime's spiritual journey, but a bit of an existential tall order at this short notice. The only advice everyone agreed on was to bring earplugs. The centre, regularly used for silent retreats, is situated immediately next to a railway line.

Now, I have a problem: I am allergic to interviews. Exposure to this allergen causes my digestive system to go on strike, my memory to liquefy and run out of my ears, and my IQ to drop by about 50 points. Questions that come out of the interviewer's mouth in perfectly standard English reach my ears as cryptic koans. If anything did emerge from my mouth 'spontaneously', I had no reason to think it would bear any resemblance to the truth, my inner feelings or the English language. I still recall with shivers telling one interview panel about my great handwriting, failing to describe my current job while being interviewed by my manager, and asking another interviewer if she could please remind me what was on my CV as I had failed to print a copy because I had the flu. The 'first thing that came into my head' would never turn up there until 20 minutes after the end of the interview. And those were jobs that asked for nothing more personal than my project management experience and customer service skills.

I had become adept at 'translating' my vocation into safe, banal generalisations for a secular audience, protecting myself from an indecent flood of emotional sincerity, but that wasn't going to cut it any more.

The Monday of the BAP arrived. I'd studied the list of selectors and potted biographies I'd received in the post, as if I might somehow deduce their line of questioning from their year of graduation or the ages of their children. I'd even resolved the all-important dilemma of what to wear, opting for the compromise candidate of jeans-and-jacket, with a range of crosses and crucifixes to cover all theological tastes.

From the moment I arrived at Shallowford House, everything felt all right. There was a genuinely prayerful and peaceful atmosphere, with sunlit gardens and sheep grazing behind the house. The 15 candidates were a fascinating illustration of God's eclectic tastes. Knowing that there was no quota and no competition, we had an immediate comradeship, breaking into loud chatter and laughter the minute we were released from the room, like kids at morning break.

Yet I did notice one odd thing about the make-up of the group. As we gathered in the chapel, I kept my eyes lowered and noticed that mine were the only shoes with heels. Several of the candidates were young men but I was the only woman under about 40—although the selectors for our group were all female. I also got the impression that young converts weren't a typical demographic; in the pastoral scenario, I had to address some 'old friends' from church who said their 20-something daughter had 'always respected' my opinion.

The most complicated bit was the meals. Each candidate is required to sit next to each of the selectors at least once, while avoiding being on the same table as somebody who has just interviewed them or is just about to, resulting in a sort of musical chairs Sudoku puzzle. But at least I felt able to eat the meals. Given my usual response to interviews, that was an unexpected bonus. And God let me know he was doing his bit. The next morning, we were to deliver our presentations, in order from one to eight according to playing cards picked from a table. I wanted to get mine out of the way first, and I knew that others wanted to avoid first or last place. That night, I dreamed of a black ace. Sure enough, the next morning, I turned over a black ace.

I found the first interviewer easy to talk to, stern but smiling. The second seemed to frown all the time except when I said anything particularly stupid, when she smiled. The third interviewer came across as really friendly and open, giving the reassuring impression that she'd heard it all before and had experienced most of it herself. I fall for that one every time.

I had only one major brain-death moment, in, of all things, the vocations interview. I could talk about my vocation all day. In fact, I talked about it for nearly the whole interview, until there was hardly any time for the other topic, which was spirituality. But then the interviewer asked: what did the Eucharist mean to me? I was stumped. How could I explain in words what even our Lord could express only through symbol and action? How could I explain what it might mean to me to hold in my created hands the Creator of the universe? Would I be able to say anything without bursting into tears? Fumbling in the sudden emptiness of my head, I managed to grab on to one thought that was too slow to flee—something my husband had said which had brought tears to my eyes. The moment I said it, I realised it sounded wrong. Anecdotes about one's husband: good small talk technique, poor interview technique. The interviewer smiled. I hoped it was in sympathy.

Still, by the end of the three days I felt quietly confident. Not confident that I'd got through, but confident that I'd been right to be there, and that I'd had an uplifting time, and that I hadn't said anything truly crashingly awful. I'd even managed to get a lift from a fellow candidate in his brand-new car.

Then we got hit by a lorry.

I heard an odd noise and looked up to see the side of a lorry far closer to the passenger window than a lorry had any business to be. I may not repeat in this book what I actually said at that moment, although it was still giving my fellow ordinand, the driver, a laugh at my expense two years later. Luckily, the lorry driver must have been woken up by our left wing mirror flying past him, because he stopped before he got as far as taking my left leg off too, and we got home unscathed (though the same could not be said for the brand-new car).

A friend of mine, recently through BAP herself, was fond of the phrase 'new level, new devil'. That is, the more you're doing God's will, the more the universe seems to be trying to shoot you down. Good to know I'm doing something right!

Waiting for
the bishop to call

Of all the waiting I'd done over the past three years, the final week was the hardest. Everything was out of my hands. The decision had been made, the report had been written, and there were at least half a dozen people who knew where I was going to be, come September, but I wasn't one of them. I felt like Schrödinger's poor cat, just waiting to find out if I was already dead.

It gave me plenty of time to reflect on the tricky subject of God's will. It's the oldest question in the book: the universe as a whole is subject to God's sovereignty, but, in isolation, lots of things happen that don't look much like anything God would want. Until now, I had been happy enough to leave that question, along with the flight mechanics of bumblebees and the wave particle duality, among the things that simply are, and are not going to be changed at all by whether I understand them or not. Now I was at the sharp end of the question. If the answer was 'yes', of course I was willing to take the risk that it was a fluke. But if it was 'no', what would that mean? That God had never wanted me to be a priest? That he had, for some reason, needed me to go to BAP and also to be turned down? Or just that the BAP had made a mistake?

Everyone else I spoke to was remarkably philosophical

about it. If it's right, it will happen. If it doesn't happen, it's not right. Everything is for the best in this best of all possible worlds. But I didn't join the Anglican Church to believe in infallibility, certainly not the infallibility of the Bishop's Advisory Panel, and even more certainly not the infallibility of the person who had provided them with the basis for their decision, since that was me.

I had confidence, though, that the situation was held within the will of God. It helps nobody to tell them that God's plan for them was always that they should be messed about for a few years and finally disappointed. Yet it is right for people to explore their vocation, and right for the church to be responsible for discerning it. God, you could say, is big on collaborative ministry. Sometimes that means we mess it up, but God still honours his promises; he has given it to his servants to minister his sacraments, and, even when they are performed imperfectly by imperfect ministers, it is his name underwriting them. I admire a good scriptwriter, one who respects the integrity of his characters rather than taking the lazy option of bending everything to fit the plot—and God is a heck of a good scriptwriter. So I trusted his imagination to cope with any unexpected plot twist. I was just impatient to find out what would happen next.

D-day. I felt slightly sorry for the bishop. In my diocese, you did not usually meet him officially in the course of the process, so this most sensitive and emotionally wrought communication might be our first and last.

I waited for the phone to ring. About four in the afternoon, I found out that there was a fault on the line. Then the internet connection went down as well. And the sound on the telly. It was like the beginning of a very low-budget horror movie. I was just waiting for the lights to start flickering, or to hear a noise in the cellar which just had to be investigated while wearing flimsy nightwear and with a suddenly unreliable torch. I'd never been much of a one for all that Old Nick stuff, but with one thing and another I was starting to get the message: God's actions in the world bring a reaction. *Something* resists. I called the diocesan secretary to give my mobile number for the bishop... and was told that nobody could see my report yet because of, guess what, technical glitches.

Eventually my phone rang. It was the bishop: 'I've got your report in front of me.' I kept my voice absolutely neutral and avoided hurrying him. It took a few minutes before I actually understood what he was saying. The decision was...

Nothing. There was no decision. The BAP had said 'No' but, he quoted, 'with reluctance'—a situation the DDO later told me he had never before encountered. My vocational journey had never been like anyone else's, and apparently my uniqueness was not yet at an end. I was baffled. The DDO was baffled. Until the BAP secretary could unbaffle us, I was going nowhere.

So it was a 'maybe', and the worst kind of 'maybe'. I should have been starting a new life, one way or another. Instead, my life was more on hold than ever. I discovered an Asian food shop on a road I often walked, and put on a stone in a month, comfort-eating on lurid green fudges and dense syrupy globes.

I'd never considered this possibility. I'd known about the bishop's right not to follow the panel's recommendation, but I'd heard it spoken of only in slightly dismissive terms—a token gesture to episcopacy, recognised as such by all except the occasional maverick bishop and no-hope candidates in denial. Friends had assured me it was, at best, embarrassing; at worst, a disadvantage to the person for the rest of their ministry.

If the bishop confirmed the panel's decision, could I really follow my plan of putting vocation aside for the time being? Could I move on with my life, knowing I'd got so close? On the other hand, if the bishop said 'Yes', I would never have that recognition by the wider church. I would always be the one with something to prove, something to apologise for. Perhaps my joy in my ministry would always be tainted. I should just save myself the embarrassment and accept it: God had given me my shot and I'd blown it.

But I came to accept that there is a role for the BAP and a role for the bishop in discerning God's will—even on the rare occasions when they seem to be at variance with one another. The criteria are there as a national standard, a safeguard against arbitrary or irresponsible decisions. The job of the selectors is to advise the bishop, based on evidence, criteria and prayerful professional judgement. It is for the bishop to be open to the possibility, once in a while, that the Spirit may be asking the church to take a risk.

When I finally received the report, for the first time I stopped feeling apologetic and started feeling angry—not angry at anyone in particular, just general omnidirectional anger, a uniform background rage at anyone and everything, including myself. I had no enemy, nobody who bore me any malice, just a group of prayerful and careful and well-intentioned Christians who had accidentally given me a slap in the face. One of the interviewers had simply misread my form. Another, in spite of my medical clearance, was concerned about my past history of depression and wanted to protect me from all the stressful aspects of ministry I'd diligently (and realistically) listed in response to her question. When the DDO spoke to the panel secretary, the response was as though they were asking me to wait a bit for something that was out of stock, not questioning my sanity and the health of my marriage. The secretary actually thought the report had been encouraging. But I didn't feel encouraged. I felt penalised for my honesty, a fool for having trusted the process. At my worst moments, I felt as if everything Jesus had given me, his Church had taken away.

I say this was 'my' report, but the main character in it seemed to be my husband. As a married woman, I'd felt all through the process that I wasn't quite being treated as an individual. My husband always seemed to be in the background of any conversation, as if they'd secretly feel more comfortable interviewing him on my behalf. When I said what I was exploring, people outside the church often asked, 'Do you want to be a bishop?'. For church people, the first question was more often, 'Is your husband a vicar?' At one conference, a woman expressed surprise that we weren't exploring ordained ministry together. Even the Examining Chaplain had assumed that my husband's liturgical tastes, rather than my own training needs, would determine where I went for curacy.

After everything I'd put my husband through, everything he'd been prepared to sacrifice for me, this was the bitterest pill. Now it's become a joke: 'The BAP thought I was in a controlling marriage', to which the response is always, 'Who's the controlling one?' But I think our marriage only survived the two weeks between my BAP report and the final decision through a silent mutual determination to pretend that we weren't thinking the obvious. Pretending it hadn't occurred to me that he was the reason my dreams had been shattered, that I was the reason he was hanging on in a job he hated, that he'd believed in me and I'd messed it up. Avoiding the conclusion that I must have said something to make them think he was overbearing, and the nagging doubt that maybe there was some truth in it. We moved round each other tenderly, constantly comforting and supporting each other, both gently avoiding asking the hard questions. If our marriage really was the barrier to my vocation, could we survive that?

The only person I wasn't angry with was God. In fact, in this whole horrible mess, he seemed to be just about the one person who hadn't had any share in it.

My spiritual director once told me that we grow most at the edges, in the wilderness, if we can just bear to hold ourselves there long enough. That was about as far as you could get from the advice I found online on 'coping with disappointment'. Search that phrase and you'll find a cheering sentiment for every disaster from losing a big contract to being diagnosed with terminal cancer. According to the latest self-help clichés, it isn't the situation that's a failure, it's your attitude to it. As one door closes, another opens: oh yes, Christians have no monopoly on that one! One website even promised that, with the right technique, I could anaesthetise my negative feelings in minutes and get on with a failure-free life.

If Christ's life and death teach us anything, it's that sometimes triumph can look like failure. But that's a million miles away from denying the reality of failure and the pain that it brings. If we believe in a world that is creation, not illusion, then pain is real. Suffering is not just the result of poor attitude. Sin is not just a valuable learning experience. Cheerfully picking ourselves up, dusting ourselves down and arming ourselves with a trite little proverb means cheating ourselves of wilderness time. I had always thought that the testing of my vocation ought to involve a little more desert and a little less tea, and I was right after all.

At first it seemed as if the only way I was growing was round my waistline. But over time, peculiarly, unexpectedly but absolutely clearly, I began to feel blessed—thankful, even. I had gone to the BAP hoping for affirmation from the panel—a 'green light' for my priestly vocation or for my continuing life as a layperson. What I had been given was the lesson that affirmation comes from God alone. I had been 'trusting in the process', letting it become everything in my life, when I should have been trusting in God.

At first I thought it would be humiliating if I only got through because the bishop set aside the recommendation of the panel. Now I see that it's exactly right. Ordination is not something earned or deserved; it's a gift. Nobody should stand at an altar and think they deserve to be there. For God to be everything in us, in ourselves we must be nothing.

At the same time, God was preparing another gift for me. I hadn't forgotten all the things I'd promised myself if I failed to get through—like writing a book and dying my hair pink. A 'yes' would mean finally saying goodbye to all the other possible lives I could have lived. Then a Christian publisher saw my blog and got in touch: if I got through, would I be interested in writing a book? Sometimes, when we give something up for God, we receive it back on a golden plate.

— ✳ —

And the pink hair? A half-failure at least deserved a half-head of pink highlights, so I booked myself in for the end of the summer. But I never kept that appointment, because a little while later, one evening when I'd stayed late at work, I got a phone call from the DDO. The bishop, he said, had 'no objection' to my starting college. I ran that sentence through my brain again. It had the word 'no' in it... but it sounded like 'yes'. I asked him to repeat it, just in case. In the absence of champagne immediately to hand, I celebrated by whizzing round the office on my desk chair, much to the amusement of my colleague, and shrieking like a little girl. A few weeks later, I was on my way to college.

The lifecycle of
the priest

In my final week at work, one of my colleagues admitted that he was intrigued to have met a 'pre-vicar'. I had become an exotic variety of wildlife, the priest in her rarely spied larval form.

In most people's experience, priests arrive fully formed, perhaps at a wedding or a Christmas carol service. Subconsciously, people assume that priests have had no previous life—hence their embarrassment and disconcertion when Father shows every sign of understanding their worldly jokes and references, for all the world as if he hadn't popped out of the womb with a dog collar already round his neck. Most people would be less surprised to hear that the church was cloning its clerics in test tubes than that their own workplace or neighbourhood might be harbouring a 'pre-vicar'.

So, for enthusiasts of esoteric wildlife, here's a brief overview of the lifecycle of the priest. You may wish to imagine this part being read by Sir David Attenborough.

The priest or cleric, in its larval form, is called an 'ordinand'. At a certain stage in its development, this grub, driven by nothing more than an instinct that it is the right thing to do, enters its chrysalis, or 'college'. There, by some hidden and magical process, it is transmuted and gains its characteristic black and white markings. The genetic make-up is identical to what it was before, but is reordered into a hitherto unforeseen beauty. In order to pass through this stage, however, the grub must first digest itself and dissolve into a rich culture medium—in other words, a living soup.

OK, I'm hoping that's stretching a metaphor a little too far.

Formation is a hidden process. The word 'seminary' means 'seed bed'. It's a place to be buried out of sight, 'hidden with Christ in God'—protected, if you like, from thorns and birds and slugs (though maybe that's a little harsh on parish life!). It's a time to concentrate on growing rather than producing fruit for harvest.

Like almost everything else I like about the church, the seminary isn't very fashionable at the moment. There are those who would prefer a 'mineral' to a 'vegetable' model of formation, knocking the rough edges off in the tumbler of the real world. As one church friend cautioned, 'You'll be out of circulation for a few years.' The alternative was to study at evenings and weekends, and carry on working up to the week before my ordination, but I'd been finding it hard enough to multitask being a Christian and a wife and a public sector office worker. If you've ever tried to think about the mechanics of how you walk as you're doing it, you'll know a little of how I felt, trying to reflect on my discipleship at the same time as trying to live it. When I've tried, I've nearly fallen over.

Moreover, I think I was a pretty good public sector office worker—better than I was a wife or a Christian, anyway. I could easily have taken off my ID badge and put on a dog collar and carried on being a pretty good public sector office worker, just with new clothes and a new job title. I needed to be taken out of the world I'd learned to live in before I met Christ, and learn to inhabit a new one. I needed to go to ground for a while—to find a safe place for some quality soup time.

— ✳ —

Laurence and I had agreed we wouldn't look at colleges until the Process was pretty far advanced. We soon found, though, that we needed to put a face to our hopes—to be able to picture our future, if 'all goes to plan', with the right geographical backdrop.

The DDO didn't hesitate in recommending three places to look at: one in Oxfordshire, one in Cambridge and one just over the Pennines in Yorkshire. I consulted others and they gave identical advice. Here at last was something everyone agreed on: those were the three colleges I should look at, coming from a liberal catholic tradition.

This was the first I'd heard that I was coming 'from' anywhere. 'Tradition' sounded richer than anything I thought I had, redolent of patina and polish. It was something to be handed down, received from family and community; a much-used, much-altered but still fully functional heirloom. For me, though, nothing was 'the way we've always done it'. All my beliefs and practices were new acquisitions, amassed from my various browsings in the junkshop of Christian culture, and still trying to find their right places on the shelves of my spiritual storeroom. Some parts of the Christian spectrum were admittedly very alien to me, but no more strange than the most familiar and cherished features of my new spirituality had been just a few years earlier. After all of the emphasis during the discernment process on transcending one's own tradition, now it seemed that everyone wanted to put me in a box—and they already knew which box I would fit.

The colleges were quite blatant in the way they labelled

themselves: 'catholic', 'liberal', 'open evangelical'. After the discreet language of the Process, it struck me as rather indecent, trumpeting our differences in public, like asking loudly at a family gathering why Uncle Eric isn't talking to Cousin Mavis. There was only one college that seemed to believe in people just getting on and being nice to one another. And so we spent a pleasant day in rural Oxfordshire, wandering in the tranquil grounds and enjoying a hearty lunch with these nice people. The setting was lovely. The people were lovely. The butterflies on the priest's vestments were lovely...

It would never work. All this niceness was too much for me: there were even children's toys in the bathroom. It was the collegiate equivalent of all-age worship. Quite apart from the possibility that I wouldn't qualify as a nice person, this felt like a stopping-off place, an educational establishment where someone already well grounded in their own tradition could pick up a degree. But I needed to find my tradition, and they didn't have one to offer.

The college in Cambridge, by contrast, was right in the town and right up my street. I could stroll to my lectures down cobbled pavements, window-shopping the quirky boutiques, perhaps picking up a flyer for a public debate. If I was going to be put in a box, this box at least was filled with clever, efficient, liberal people. A current student assured me that there was no place here for anyone I would disagree with over women or gay people. (Not that Anglicans spend all their time talking about gender and sex. We disagree about lots of other things too.) But I wasn't sure that was the kind of safety I was looking for.

That wasn't the only kind of segregation going on. Theological colleges, unlike any other British university, have no standard entry requirements. Ordinands may have a doctorate, an O Level or nothing at all; their last essay might have been written last year or last century. At this college, applicants were carefully sieved and graded into half a dozen different courses from two different universities. Boxes within boxes. When I picked up my glossy prospectus and DVD, I had no shortage of assistance from students eager to explain why their course was the most demanding or the best taught, or offered the most realistic preparation for ministry. It was so difficult to make my mind up that it was easier not to go there at all. I'd just spent the last five years unlearning that kind of intellectual combativeness. I would have felt right at home, and that was no good at all.

Mirfield was different. For a start, they didn't have an open day. They certainly didn't have a glossy prospectus. In fact, they were barely in the telecommunications age at all. My emails were lost in the ether, the telephone number was unrecognised, and even good old Royal Mail mislaid my letter for an entire month. But by this time, these kind of hitches had started to seem less like obstacles and more like familiar wayposts marking the right path. What Mirfield does have is monks, and perhaps, in important spiritual respects, that gives it a connectivity that a mere broadband cable does not provide.

When I arrived, I was at once informed that I had an interview. This came as a slight surprise, since I wasn't aware I'd made an application. The interview was conducted by a monk, whose bookshelf included such popular classics as *Estonian Ecumenism* and the complete works of Bernard of Clairvaux in a German edition, and who terrified me by peppering the conversation with references to African cities and English biblical scholars that I was sure to have heard of.

Luckily, my poor memory for names (and places, and facts) turned out to my advantage when I innocently praised an excellent book I'd recently read... written by the interviewer. I mentioned that it was the only modern book that didn't make me feel out of kilter with the church. They sent me an acceptance letter without even waiting for my application form.

This is a place where silence has soaked into the stones, where time passes in centuries—a place where the latest battles over finances and structures and strategies are a distraction from a more eternal battle that can only be fought on one's knees. The introduction I was given gave an impression of asceticism: a six-day week, two compulsory and two optional services daily, silence at breakfast and after 9.30 pm, and a bar that was open (my heart sank) 'every Thursday evening'. There was no eagerness here to compete for my application: 'The best year', my interviewer reminisced, 'was when we had seven students.'

But even seven students looked optimistic for that year. Everybody I met made it their business to warn me against Mirfield. I got used to a certain response—a look of slight alarm and the words 'not a happy place'. The college had just lost its 100-year-old link with the University of Leeds, and the glorious church was closed for a controversial restoration and reordering. On the day I was due to meet the principal, he resigned. I don't normally have quite that drastic an effect.

The opinion of friends and advisers was clear: Cambridge was prestigious, intellectually challenging, altogether the obvious choice for a student of my calibre. And yet... that same night at Mirfield, the students took it in turns, trudging in their black cassocks across the white snow to the empty and unheated church, for a 24-hour vigil of prayer. I had promised at my baptism to hold out against sin, the world and the devil, and here was a fortress under siege.

Cambridge was the safe choice. Mirfield was an insane risk. When you put it like that, there was no competition.

And that was how, dear reader, your comfortable grass-fed Cheshire ordinand and her southern Jessie husband came to make the intrepid trek across the Pennines to what we hoped would indeed be God's own country.

The college found us a house very close to the college, in Battyeford—which, now I was a local, I quickly learned I should always pronounce as Batty Ford, never Battifud. This would be called a suburb of Mirfield, were it not so absurd to describe as 'urban' a town that still has half-day closing on a Thursday. Still, it was well equipped for the rather singular needs of the local community. The dry cleaners offers a special price on cassocks, and the mini Co-op had a special offer on vegan ready-meals throughout Lent.

For what was supposed to be a retreat from the world, moving house proved to be more 'real world' than anything else I'd experienced during the process. The only thing we had to show for five years of settled grown-up life was enough clutter to require our first ever removal van. And so—thankfully, at the expense of the diocese—I got a crash course in the logistics of moving house. I found out what a 'wardrobe box' is—namely, a wreckage of cardboard and twisted metal from which clothes are excavated. I learned what the requirements are for installing a washing machine, and that we didn't have them. I made the acquaintance of Pledge Dusting Cloths, and, for a while, they made a serious bid for being my favourite thing in the universe.

I also had to brush up on some subjects I hadn't studied since secondary school—such as mathematics, for doing battle with the impenetrable church finance forms. Work out three-quarters of your partner's income less essential expenditure multiplied by the first number you thought of and add two if your initial measurement was an even number. Written comprehension: can 'Your rent will be included in the payment from the diocese' be read to mean 'Your rent will be taken into account in the means-tested assessment of your payment from the diocese'? Yes, it can—although it would have been helpful to realise this before we signed for the house. I hadn't counted on being a kept woman.

Finally came the moment, late one evening after the shops had shut, when all our worldly possessions were safely in Yorkshire. We, on the other hand, were stranded in Cheshire, with no corkscrew, no glasses, and nothing to toast our fifth wedding anniversary but a bottle of Advocaat. Advocaat out of a plastic cup is perhaps an acquired taste, but one I recommend you develop. You never know when you might need it.

Part 2

First impressions

It is a universal fact of Freshers' Week that you will get a *Friends* title. You know how it works: 'the one with...'.

When I went up to university the first time round, I got my Freshers' Week name on the first day: 'the one with the tiger-print trousers'. (This was 2001. I have no excuse.) Once it became apparent that I had more than one pair of trousers, and that this was therefore an unreliable means of identification, I turned into 'the one with very long hair'. This worked fine until my third year when I had it all cut off and my friends started blanking me in the street.

After this experience, as you might imagine, I was anxious to make the right first impression at my theological college. Something like 'the smart, friendly, quirky, not actually self-obsessed one' would do—quite difficult to communicate with just a smile and the right choice of glasses. I needn't have worried. The first fellow student I met identified me straight away: 'You're the one with the blog.'

My initiation into the strange world that is theological college started even before we arrived. Part of formation is about learning to inhabit a new role; learning to see ourselves, and be seen by others, as something different. It is, if you like, a makeover.

When it came to ordering my cassock, I thought it would be pretty much 'black, size 14'. Oh no. There are more options on a cassock than on a Starbucks latte. Mine's a double-breasted wool worsted three centre pleats closed collar added cuffs side slits and easy on the soya milk. The questions on the order form were possibly the hardest I'd been asked in the whole discernment process: height *front and back*? Not to mention the personal questions about the gracefulness or otherwise of my gait and posture. I had enough anxieties about how I was going to measure up to the demands of ministerial training; now I was also worried about whether my ears lined up with my shoulder seams.

In the words of St Paul, there is one body but many members—and I had to give measurements for every flipping one of them. A few days later, a kindly seamstress phoned me up and explained gently that the figures I'd submitted didn't add up to the shape of a human being. Would I perhaps like some help with the measuring?

However, my fears that all this precision would result in some embarrassingly figure-hugging little black number proved unfounded. The cassock makers have many years' experience of working with theological colleges. When my cassock arrived, I found they'd left ample room to accommodate three years of enforced cake (of which more later) and essay-induced comfort-eating. It was also fully fitted out with all the tricks of the vestment trade. There are slits to get at your trouser pockets (many is the clergyman who has found himself scrabbling under his skirts to turn on a radio mic at the start of his sermon, all because he neglected to consider trouser-pocket access); cuffs big enough to accommodate a pen, an order of service and the entire *Summa Theologica* of Thomas Aquinas; and a sort of fringe or brush on the inside of the hem that made me feel a bit like a vacuum cleaner, but clearly showed I'd got a superior product. And the cloak! Perfect for Hallowe'en, medieval fayres and Harry Potter conventions. It even has concealed pockets on either side, just about the right size for Bombay Sapphire bottles. A swooshy cloak may seem like a self-indulgence, but think of it as an investment—insurance against all future last-minute fancy dress party invites.

I might not have a clue what I was doing here, but at least I looked the part.

The day here starts at 7.30 with Mattins, six days out of seven, and ends with Evensong or, optionally, Compline. On the feast days of the most prestigious saints, the ones who get maximum scores on saintly Top Trumps, Mattins is pushed back a full half-hour to 8.00 am, followed by a cooked breakfast. I experienced my first major saint's day in my first week at college; the delight with which the second- and third-year students treasured that extra half-hour in bed ought perhaps to have been a warning of the exhaustion to come.

The monastic service books are the product of decades of liturgical scholarship, much fraternal wrangling, and a photocopier. Never before had I had cause to ask in a choir practice, 'Which page 67 are we on?' Another favourite to catch out first-years is the instruction 'Turn to page 50'… written on page 50. I like to imagine some overliteral student stuck in a perpetual loop, unable to complete the service and condemned to stare for ever at page 50.

Still, at least there *is* a book. You have something in front of you, in black and white. In theory you know what it is you're meant to do. At the 'second table', you're on your own.

If the 'first table' is the altar, the 'second table' is what we like to call the communal meals. Being able to choose when and where to eat is one of the basic things that most of us take for granted. It's part of the autonomy that comes with being an adult: children have to eat what's put in front of them; adults have control of their own kitchen. But that became my first sacrifice to communal living. The first time I cooked in three months was on Christmas Day. I was in charge of roast potatoes, and they came out like lumps of coal, left by Santa for a naughty girl.

Food is an important part of ordained ministry. While not every priest ends up eating four Christmas dinners like the Vicar of Dibley, during your ordained ministry you will certainly be called on to eat large quantities of homemade cake, sausage rolls and supermarket nibbles, all in the call of duty. I had never known what it was to physically crave vitamins until I went on parish placement. But the busy parish priest is not just being polite as they tuck into that egg and cress muffin or Asian snack selection. The minutes they've saved from their schedule by not cooking could be the difference between being well prepared for the funeral tomorrow and checking the deceased's name on their phone on the way to the crem. I've known priests who live on nothing but cup-a-soup, coffee, gin and the occasional bring-and-share quiche. They could be one parish function away from starvation.

So laying down your fat reserves at college is simple efficiency—and food has a spiritual as well as a purely calorific value. Food means fellowship, hospitality, mutual service. Following the monastic tradition of work and prayer, we all take our turn in serving food and washing up (although, also following the monastic tradition, the aim is our spiritual growth rather than practical effectiveness. Anything requiring genuine skill, such as cooking and gardening, is left to the professionals). And food means feast and fast, fish on Fridays and sausages for saints. If abstinence is a duty, so too, at the appropriate time, is celebration. If you are what you eat, we are literally metabolising the liturgical calendar.

And so, alongside the daily round of spiritual sustenance from the monastic offices comes the bodily sustenance, which is observed with the same sense of tradition and quasi-liturgical propriety—cake at 11.00, freshly brewed coffee in the Common Room each evening, and woe betide anybody who thinks to clear away their plate before the principal gives the signal. In the 'common life', hurrying to get to the pudding before others would be distinctly Bad Form. Significant glances at those who are tarrying over the main course are, however, permitted.

Breakfast here is silent, so there is nothing to do except eat my food and try not to stare too closely at how the person opposite eats theirs. One guy eats a red apple, cutting it into tidy mouth-sized pieces. One has created his own customised cereal by mixing cornflakes and muesli. Another is engaged in a lengthy construction project involving toast, peanut butter, jam and a banana. I am destroying a soft piece of toast with a hard piece of butter and demonstrating the original purpose of the 'scapular' we wear—that is, as a bib. I have never felt more conspicuous in my life.

To the novice, the whole thing is like some sadistic social experiment. *Big Brother* meets *The Monastery*: 30 people attempt to complete arbitrary challenges without the benefit of direct communication. Everything works on unwritten rules, and, by the end of the second week, I had deduced only one rule: everything Katy does is wrong. I was even called a heretic in my second theology lecture, by the lecturer.

Outwardly, my ordinand disguise seemed convincing, but even that fell apart the moment I encountered stairs. On the paths, we float along, 21 black cassocks against the green grass and the white October sky. Then we reach the steps and I come to an abrupt halt. I never thought I would have sympathy with a dalek. Goodbye proto-clergywoman, gliding serenely as a vacuum cleaner; hello giant crane fly in a binbag, all elbows and knees and flailing black cloth.

Well, they do say that going to theological college is supposed to be deskilling. I can't cook, I can't eat, I can't even walk up stairs any more. I'm obviously making great progress already.

The cassock wasn't the only new outfit I brought with me to college. One day, God willing, I would be a priest—but first I was going to be a student again. So I plucked up my courage, tried to forget I wasn't a willowy pale teenager, and took a trip round the quirky little vintage boutiques that I hadn't been cool enough for in my first student days. I still wasn't cool enough, just old enough not to care. As I had once celebrated the end of my childhood by buying those identity-defining tiger-print trousers, so now I celebrated the end of my adulthood (or, at least, its temporary suspension) by spending my final pay cheque as a UK taxpayer on silly little indie dresses.

I'd been advised that most ordinands react to being 'mature students' in one of two ways. Some resent the experience of deskilling, of losing the professional status and identity they've had for perhaps the past 20 or 30 years. There are theological students, and even some priests, who never pass up an opportunity to remind you that they 'are' a teacher or a social worker or an engineer, when actually they're an ordinand just like you. Then there are those who embrace the student label wholeheartedly. Hitherto responsible adults, with years of being sensible as professionals and parents, joyfully fling off the burdens of their past lives and employ the wisdom of their greater years on a bigger-budget remake of their student days.

I had a lot of sympathy with those who missed their jobs. Having been selected for everything they could bring to ordained ministry, now they were here no attempt was made to recognise or make use of their existing skills. People who had been experts were now beginners, as clueless as the rest of us newbies. Fifty-something businessmen were being shown the ropes by the 23-year-old postgrad down the corridor. For a recent graduate like me, deskbound and given to abstraction at the best of times, 'theology student' was a pretty comfortable self-definition. But for someone who had spent the past couple of decades building houses or designing cars, and could take pride in being more interested in the tensile strength of a pin than how many angels might currently be dancing on its head, it must've been a shock to follow God's call to be a priest and find themselves instead as a humanities student.

Rather complacently (in retrospect), I thought I could avoid the pitfalls of both categories. I was thankful that I'd never had a career to speak of and was rarely tempted to slip into conversation, 'I'm a data protection expert.' But I also assumed that I could safely embrace the college experience without losing the maturity and professionalism I'd gained over the past five years. At 24, I'd enjoyed being a professional woman with pencil skirts and a business card. Now I was approaching 30, it was rather a bonus to find myself once more a Young Person and with a railcard to prove it. Plus, I'd made a pretty pathetic job of being a student the first time round, if being a student is supposed to involve reckless excess. All my sex, drugs and rock 'n' roll had been squeezed into a rather efficient and focused six months of hedonism, safely far from any exam period. The rest of the time, I'd been highly studious, periodically teetotal and addicted to nothing more extreme than instant coffee and mince pies.

I had obviously learned from those mistakes.

One of the happiest moments of my time at theological college was getting ID'd buying wine in the Co-op shortly after my 30th birthday. My most shameful was shaking all through the Armistice Day service the morning after the night before, and wondering whether this was what dying of alcohol poisoning felt like—while a young chap with whom I'd been knocking back the Shiraz, and who I knew for a fact had been dancing the hokey-cokey and singing favourites from the English Hymnal into the early hours, looked as if he'd had eight hours' sleep and a facial. A 30-year-old metabolism is just not up to a 19-year-old's lifestyle.

There was one moment when I did get a twinge about being a student again. I took my little sister out to dinner and, when I went to pay the bill, she pointed out that she should be the one subbing me, since she'd just started on a junior doctor's salary. Now in my mind she will always be about seven (can you imagine, they let primary school kids be doctors now!). Losing status in the world was no big deal; losing the status of big sister in my own family was something different. It did feel, briefly, as if the past ten years of my life had been a false start; I'd failed in Adult Life and had been sent back to the age of 18 to re-take.

— ✳ —

I pretty quickly learned to accept gracefully the generosity of others, though. Being spoiled by my old friends I now look on as something of a perk.

And I can't help thinking I've had the best of it. Just before I started at college, I went up to my old university for a reunion (I couldn't understand what the occasion was until someone reminded me that it'd been ten years since I started there) and I realised I was the one living the dream. The person on my left spent most of the evening telling me about the well-paid job he hated. At college, in the simplest way, I was just doing what I loved. For one thing, I was around other people who actually enjoyed going to church. We even had an occasional Benediction and Curry Club, touring northern towns on the lookout for decent liturgy. Suddenly church services weren't a slightly embarrassing Sunday morning pastime, but a treat to be approached with gourmet enthusiasm.

Practice makes perfect. By the end of my first term, I had learned the art of operating the cassock—the graceful gather when going upstairs, the deft manoeuvre when sitting at the start of the service so that you don't get throttled the first time we all bow. Now I could move on to the advanced lesson—walking upstairs with a bottle of wine in one hand and a glass in the other. I marked up my service books with colour-coded tabs (stationery really is the answer to everything). I stopped being confused when people asked 'How was your weekend?' first thing on Sunday morning, and started referring to the apostles as Sausage Saints. I even felt irritated if some visiting group disturbed the serenity of my silent breakfast. In other words, I had absorbed 'the Mirfield Way'!

I threw myself into college life and didn't look back. Within a couple of weeks, my old workplace—the offices where I'd worked for five years—had joined the house my parents had when I was little and the examination hall of my old university as nothing more than a stage set for night-time dreams. Even my old church felt like part of a different world I'd left behind. When people asked, 'Where's home?' I looked confused and said, 'Here!'

For the past three years I'd been living in the future. Now that the future was actually going to happen, ironically I wasn't thinking about it at all. I was happy just to live in the present, to concentrate on learning and changing and experiencing it all. In spite of the long hours, I had never had so much energy. I hardly needed to sleep. Most of all, I had the enormous, rare luxury of knowing that right now I was exactly where I was meant to be.

> *'Tis the gift to be simple, 'tis the gift to be free,*
> *'tis the gift to come down where you ought to be...*
> JOSEPH BRACKETT (1848)

77

Underpaid, underprepared and undergraduate

I guess not many of my fellow ordinands went to the same hairdresser as me, because when I said I was studying theology, she asked, 'What's theology?'

Good question.

The most accurate answer is that theology is the knowledge of God, and therefore not really an academic subject in the sense that it can be fully learned in the library or in the lecture hall. If to be a theologian is to 'pray truly', then we're here to learn enough about who it is we're praying to that we don't find ourselves worshipping our own mental images and distortions.

In practical terms, theology is not really one subject. It's about four or five. As well as systematics (what you might call philosophical theology or doctrine), there's biblical studies, liturgy, church history, and mission and ministry. It's very different from my studies of history, where the various modules and papers were all pretty much 'stuff that happened in the past'. As for biblical studies, that just means studies that have one thing in common—the Bible. Turn up to a biblical studies lecture and you have no way of knowing whether you're about to get historical-critical, literary, linguistic, feminist, confessional or post-colonial. My first tutor in biblical studies, an eccentric and atheistic old prof with a white moustache and a canvas hat, who didn't look 'post'-colonial at all, told us that he hated history and that the Bible would be entirely boring if the events of the Old Testament had actually happened.

One recognised possible side effect of studying theology is losing your faith. At traditional Catholic seminaries, students are not even allowed to start studying theology for at least the first year of their course. Theology is strong medicine. The temptation for us was to protect ourselves, to treat the course as just another hoop to jump through before getting ordained. Even I felt uneasy. You might think that a critical approach to faith would hold no terrors for me. After all, I used to eat Christians for breakfast. It wasn't as if the problem of suffering or the varying accounts of the four Gospels were going to come as a terrible surprise to me. If anybody tried to challenge my faith, I would probably be tempted to interrupt and take over their side of the argument, knowing that I could make their case better than they could. But that didn't mean my faith could not be threatened by theology. I knew that God did not owe it to me to be nice or sympathetic or the way I wanted him to be. I needed to encounter the scriptures as they are, in the fullness of their diversity and difficulty, and allow *them* to interpret *me*. I had to get to know God—and he might turn out to be very different from who I thought he was.

The first essay I handed in was entitled 'What kind of language can possibly speak to us of the mystery of God?' A neat little poser, I think you'll agree, which I was supposed to have all tied up in 1000 words.

When I say 'handed in', what I actually did was upload it to an application called Turnitin, which automatically anonymised it, checked the word count, ran a comparison against the internet and everybody else's essays and came back with a 'plagiarism score'. If the traffic light was green, it meant either that your work was brilliantly original or that you hadn't actually read any books. When I was an undergraduate, back in a more innocent pre-Wikipedia age, we just queued up and gave it in. When I was an undergraduate *the first time*, I should say. Now here I was, baffled by 'semesters' and 'continuous assessment' and the electronic self-service machines in the library, muttering about how it was 'in my day...' and feeling like a very 'mature' student indeed.

I had forgotten just how infuriating it was to be an undergraduate. Writing with *footnotes*! Manipulating word counts. Being a student ID number, not a free man. The liturgical arcana of the church has nothing to compare with the ritual of formatting according to the *Usus* of Sheffield University. That first essay—which was only about the length of a footnote from some of the books I'd had to read—took longer to format than to write. It might not prepare me for preaching but I was going to be a whizz at the PCC minutes.

It was all strangely disempowering. Until now, I'd had the normal authority of any layperson, which is to say, the right to express my beliefs, restricted only by my willingness or otherwise to get into a fight. This is, after all, the age of the blog and the BBC News comments section, where we are all entitled to be as wrong as we like. Now suddenly I didn't have the right to an opinion unless it was fully referenced, properly spaced and surrounded by 2.5 cm margins.

When I discussed my essay title with others, everybody had a suggestion: song, or art, or liturgy, or the language of salvation. 'I might just make it up,' I told my tutor over coffee, in a moment of ill-advised candour. After all, I reasoned, we all have experience of trying to talk about God, and none of us will know who got closest until that blessed day when there will be an end of all theology and particularly of all essays. She made me to understand that this was a Very Bad Idea. The purpose of an essay, she reminded me, is not to come up with my own answer, no matter how brilliant (my tutor kindly refrained from pointing out how unlikely this would be), but to show that I can engage with the academic debate.

So I spent weeks reading detailed analyses about the difference between analogy and metaphor, their respective merits and demerits, their relationship to parables and paradigms, and how simile is just out of the game entirely. What I learned, I found surprisingly relevant to my faith. And yet... Where was song? Where was language about salvation? Where were art and liturgy? Where, in fact, were the things laypeople and working priests were asking? And why was I writing an essay to prove to an audience of one that I'd read the right books, rather than trying to find answers to the questions of the church and the world? Because I was an undergraduate, that's why.

When I came out of my final exam at university, I promised myself I would never do another exam in my life. Nothing, but nothing, was worth that level of stress. No matter what else life might have in store for me—pass or fail, career or unemployment, marriage or divorce—there was one thing that made my whole future look bright: no more exams ever.

Ha! In fact, within a couple of years I'd taken a professional qualification, involving an exam, just because it was being offered at work. The truth is, studying gets to be a bit of an addiction. A few years later, here I was taking a whole other degree.

I'd set myself the aim of doing 'just well enough'. Every point over 60 per cent was a point wasted—effort that could have been spent on prayer, or sleep, or beer. In this aim, I failed hopelessly. I'd chosen my college partly because I felt it didn't prioritise academic success over the things that really matter. Unfortunately, I do. You get marks for essays; you do not get marks for sanctity—and writing essays, unlike holiness of life, is something that comes pretty naturally to me. I sometimes think I specialise in the kind of talents that impress people very much but for which they aren't prepared to actually give me any money. Joined-up handwriting, for instance. Back in primary school, the handwriting class was my top subject; I was utterly deflated to discover that at secondary school *there was no handwriting class*. In the same way, essay writing is not a skill in much demand in the real world, and certainly not one that anyone's prepared to pay for (except for a few notionally legal websites that keep Turnitin busy). But if you're never going to have fame and fortune, a nice fat number in the top right-hand corner of your essay is a very easy substitute temptation.

It turns out that writing essays is one of those things you get better at just by getting older. It's like swimming and cooking. My teachers and I endured years of lessons which only served to confirm in everyone's mind that I would never be any good at either. But several years later, without having done anything to hone my skills except spend more time on this earth, I had somehow become passably competent. It would have saved us all a lot of time and aggro if I'd skipped the lessons and come back when I was old enough to be some good. When it came to writing essays, I had the rare privilege of being able to do exactly that: to go back and have a second crack at an undergraduate degree. But I hadn't counted on how my standards would have changed over five years as a professional. I couldn't write 'pretty good for a 19-year-old' any more. By the time I'd read enough on analogy and metaphor to think I might be beginning to understand it, I'd probably read enough for a Master's course, supposing I had been at a sufficiently undiscriminating university and knew the examiner's favourite brand of whisky.

In a spirit of comradeship, we all made the mistake of sharing our first essay marks. Of course, this set, for the rest of our time at college, the reputations we had to live up (or possibly down) to. As one fellow student said, 'You'll get an even better mark next time'. Oh dear.

If there's one thing everyone knows about clergy, it's that we preach sermons. In fact, I bet if you were to ask them what they think we do at 'vicar school', most people would say we learn how to preach sermons.

If we do, it's mostly by a process of elimination. Once you've learned that your favourite illustration of the Trinity is heretical, that your favourite letter of Paul is not by Paul, and that your favourite saint never actually existed except as a typographical error in some monastic manuscript, then you're just grateful if you survive the slalom of sermon writing without slamming into any mistakes which would get you burned at the stake by the Inquisition/Sheffield Department of Biblical Studies (delete as appropriate).

I'm glad to say that none of us have lost our faith through

studying theology, but I think we are at risk of losing the ability to talk about our faith. Most people seem to leave college believing pretty much what they did when they arrived but a lot more aware of all the ways in which people could misunderstand it.

In my previous life, I worked for a public sector body, providing guidance on the application of a particular (notorious) piece of legislation. It wasn't very easy. The problem was that we were all experts. For every general rule, we knew exceptions. For every illustration that seemed straightforward at first sight, our overeducated imaginations could dream up scenarios in which the opposite would be the case. We knew all these details and we couldn't unknow them. So something that was 'true' to the general user, who took it at face value, became 'false' to us.

Hence the preacher's fear. The truth of God goes far beyond what we can express, but if every heresy is a partial truth, every partial truth could get someone calling me a heretic. And it really is not possible to put footnotes in a sermon. Trinity Sunday is the classic example. I lose track of how many times I've heard a preacher start their Trinity Sunday sermon with a comment such as 'I drew the short straw' or 'Normally I go on holiday on Trinity Sunday' or some similarly humorous expression of terror. It's probably intended to relax the congregation. It doesn't.

This attitude always used to annoy me. It seemed designed to reinforce the prejudice that the Trinity is 'just a doctrine', an obscure academic formula to be memorised (or, more likely, forgotten) rather than a life-giving reality to enter into. I'm glad to find that the study of theology has enhanced rather than deadened my passion for the Trinity, but I do now have some sympathy for those preachers. I'm not sure

I'd preach about the Trinity any differently from the way I would have done before—but I'd make perfectly sure there weren't any ordinands in the congregation.

The very first time I had to preach, I started thinking about the texts while on the bus and had written the whole thing by the time I reached my destination. Call it divine inspiration, call it beginner's luck, call it a really slow journey on the 85 to Chorlton. 'So that's how sermons happen!' I thought. 'That's good to know!' When I came to my second sermon, then, I confidently waited to receive it. It didn't happen. And then I realised with horror: I am going to have to write this thing myself, and I have absolutely no idea where to start.

I still don't. I've approached every sermon in a completely different way. I think they've come out well, but how would I know? Most feedback from listeners falls into one of three categories: (1) generic compliment, (2) profound but incomprehensible comment on something you didn't say, and, by far the most popular, (3) volume-related. At one placement, my fellow student and I received identical feedback, with one qualification: 'He is too loud; she is too quiet.'

It is best to see the production of a sermon as a battle of God's law versus Murphy's law. Anything that can be misplaced will disappear; technology that was in perfect working order five minutes before will mysteriously break down. At the same placement, the two of us led what was meant to be a meditative Lenten service of music, images and silence, which, due to technological failures, became a service of mostly just silence. Anything short of complete paranoia is wanton complacency. Be prepared. Be very prepared.

So far, the lessons I have learned about preaching are as

follows. Make sure your car has been serviced recently. Do not bring visual aids that are breakable. Do not swap cassocks with someone, leaving your sermon in their pocket. On the other hand, do not try to avoid this pitfall by not wearing a cassock or not having any pockets. Microphones need somewhere to go, and a yard of wiring down your bodice can really put you off your stride.

All but one of those lessons was learned in a single sermon—and I am very grateful to the fabulous congregation, for whom I will have to add a whole other category of feedback: (4) hugs! Next time I hear a sermon, I think I shall have to say, 'Nice sermon, vicar! I particularly liked the bit where you turned up to the right church and had the sermon with you. Do you want a hug?'

After two years of 'theological studies', I can hardly consider myself a theologian, one with the knowledge of God. In fact, I am told that the whole Orthodox Church has produced only two people it considers worthy of that title: Gregory 'the theologian' Nazianzus, and Symeon 'the new theologian'. What I did have was a piece of paper saying that I had grown in the knowledge and love of God to the level of a BA degree.

I spent results day at the local university chaplaincy, handing out cake and sympathy and refraining from sharing the wisdom of my greater years—that getting a degree is not really a big deal. I remember what it was like the first time—three years living, eating and breathing the university world. It was an era; it was my whole adult life to that date. I arrived a schoolgirl, my experience of 'the world, the flesh and the devil' consisting of a couple of dates with my gay friend and his ex-girlfriend (it's complicated) and a miserable fortnight as an exchange student somewhere near Montpellier. I left as an engaged woman. More happened in my life in those three years than in the previous 18, and getting my degree was the culmination of all of it. This was pass or fail on my whole life. No wonder the students at the chaplaincy needed cake.

This time round, the degree felt more like a side effect. None of us were present for our graduation; I found out that I was a graduate (again) when somebody posted it on Facebook. By the time the final results came through, most people in my year had already gone through a far more important change of status than that of undergraduate to graduate. When you're ordained you're ordained, and there's no such thing as an Upper-Second-Class priest.

There's another reason why I wasn't so excited—and another thing I didn't share with the new graduates at the chaplaincy. When I graduated in history, I felt that I was 'qualified'—an authority in my subject, having earned my entrance into the adult world of work. What I quickly found was that my qualification and other people's expectations didn't match up. Family members and acquaintances expected me to know the date of every historical event. Employers expected experience, or at least a further work-specific qualification. There was not a single history-related job for which my 'qualification' actually qualified me.

'Cleric' or 'clergy' means an educated person, but there's a limit to how *clericus* you can get in just two or three years. In practice, we can get only a taste of each area of theology, a sort of mezze platter of subjects. If the reading for the day happens to come from Genesis or the letter to the Ephesians, I'm your man. If it's Isaiah or Romans, then it's back to Professor Google. So I'm under no illusions that I am an 'expert' in theology and biblical studies. I don't even have GCSE RE. I've already been teased about not knowing the order of the biblical books: 'And you're the one studying theology!'

A life more common

A few years earlier, I had felt uncomfortable even going into a church. Now I was living in an all-Christian environment. I had no idea what to expect; the only thing I thought I could be sure of was that society within these walls would be entirely different from that outside.

I hoped it would be like a three-year retreat, an extended spa day for the soul, a chance to wallow in scented silences or invigorate my spirit with the athletic disciplines of prayer. The renovated church, nearing completion in my first term, even looked like a luxury health spa—all tiles and glossy marble, with the underfloor heating sauna-hot under my toes. What I feared was that it would be more like three years at a badly led house group, being nice about other people's opinions, keeping quiet about my own, with nothing more stimulating to look forward to than a second Bourbon biscuit with my tea.

But one advantage of a catholic college is that, let's just say, over-niceness is not a problem (and gin doesn't go very well with Bourbon biscuits). As for stimulants, I seem to have taken up passive smoking. It's cheap, it's sociable, and you get to keep the moral high ground—and carcinogenic particles, like everything else in our life together, are meant to be shared. This is the Common Life.

— ✳ —

There are few other contexts in modern British life in which people are thrown together quite so closely as at a college like this. The armed forces are the only parallel I can think of: there's slightly less in the way of mortal danger (we're more concerned with immortal dangers here) but otherwise it's scarily similar. In my previous life, I knew most people only in one context: they were my colleagues or my neighbours or my friends or folks from church. I knew them, but I knew one side of them, and they knew one side of me. In college, we don't just live together or just work together. The people I study with are the same people I eat with, the same people I pray with, the same people I socialise with. We get the 360-degree Google Streetview perspective.

Perhaps this is what 'communities' used to be like, when everyone went out to the same fields to work and repaired to the same pub of an evening. Nowadays, the word 'community' is overused: just because I sleep in the same postcode as somebody, it doesn't really make me part of their community. The words 'close-knit community' are most commonly followed by '… has been shocked by the murder'. Come to think of it, after three years of the Common Life, that shouldn't surprise me one bit.

The thing that gets forgotten about community is just how physical it is. We're used to online communities, to friends on Facebook and family on the phone. But the Common Life means, bluntly, that you can never get away from each other. This is especially true at morning prayer. Whether you like it or not, you're going to be spending that fragile pre-caffeine time of the morning squeezed into rather a small space with a bunch of other people who are feeling equally hypersensitive. Any noticeable and persistent habit at this time of the morning (Sings Enthusiastically, Turns Up Late, Gets the Giggles or Noisy Heels) will immediately be magnified into your defining characteristic and the bane of somebody else's life.

When you sit in the same seat in chapel every morning, next to the same people, there's a different kind of intimacy from the intimacy of long conversations—an unchosen, perhaps unwelcome intimacy of space and sound and, not to put too fine a point on it, smell. If you had a late night curry, your neighbour can see the bags under your eyes, they can hear your stomach rumbling, and they'd better like garlic. If Christianity is an embodied faith, this is incarnational living. And if your brothers and sisters in Christ seem to be coming down with a nasty bug, don't worry too much about how to work up that pastoral sympathy. Wait until tomorrow and you'll really be able to say, 'I know just how you feel.' Like the early Christians, we have all things in common, especially the common cold.

The result is, though, that you actually get to know people. You don't necessarily know much *about* them: there are people I've lived alongside for a year or more who still surprise me by left-field revelations such as a sibling or their place of birth. You just know them, know what makes them tick, what makes them collapse in giggles during Evensong, and what makes them bite your head off. There's a kind of comradeship that transcends simply liking or getting on with people.

One of the ways this shows itself is in the breaking down of the normal boundaries that apply with non-family members. People answer the door in the nude or shout 'Come in!' from their beds or bathrooms. By the end of my first term, it seemed perfectly normal to hold hands on the way back from the pub or engage in a group hug. When I arrived at college, I was still Smart Casual girl, straightening my hair every morning before Mattins and bringing my heels into college in a bag. That lasted about two weeks. By the end of the first term, I just turned up with wet hair. Time was, when the only way to see my naked face was to wake up with me; after a few months in an institution with no eligible males, make-up just seems like a waste of hard-earned Boots Advantage points. Occasionally I see snooty articles about mums turning up to school or to Tesco's in their PJs, but have you ever considered what might be under your priest's cassock at the early morning service?

Priests, at least according to the theory, are not 'trained' but 'formed'. The theory of formation is that people don't learn to be good priests (or, indeed, good people) primarily by learning certain principles and choosing to follow them, but by imbibing the culture of the community in which they live. It's the relationships we have, the norms we are exposed to, that determine how we are likely to act. So much of our cultural tradition, whether it's in a college or in the church, is reliant on unspoken personal transmission from one generation to the next. So it's things like eating together, which seems to waste so much time, that are really all-important—situations in which we are forced to be attentive to one another and to 'how things are done' round here.

That chain is easily broken and difficult to re-establish. I guess, if you were to start with a stable community of genuinely holy people (or even just reasonably functional ones), they might indeed pass on their good habits. But what we have in college is a very rapid turnover of people; it's not unusual to have more new people arriving for the start of the new year than there are people staying from the previous year. Until the beginning of my second year, I assumed that the college community would continue from one year to the next and would simply add and incorporate new members. Wrong. For the first few days of my second year, I kept catching myself thinking, 'When's it going to be back to normal?' or 'This can't last; we'll be back to normal soon.' I even tried substituting one person for another—X is the new Y—until I identified somebody as the new me and realised I wasn't quite ready to be replaced. But the community that existed in my first year *no longer existed*. It had been replaced by a new community, of which I was just as much a new member as any of the first years. Each member is essential to the community; change one person and you have a new community. So it only takes a few people following each other—'the blind leading the blind'—to establish a whole new custom. Suddenly, bowing after Evensong (for instance) is 'what the college does'. Nobody has made a decision, and yet 'the way we do things round here' has changed. It's particularly unsettling to old hands when that is exactly what was considered the *wrong* way two years previously.

Living in community is probably one of the most amazing, privileged experiences a person can have. But it's tough—tougher than you'd imagine a life with daily cake could possibly be.

Living in college, you learn a lot about people and about community. You learn about different personality types and how to live with them. You learn that whatever one person loves, another person will hate. You learn that people's perceptions of the same event can be polar opposites, and that this says more about their personalities than about what actually happened. It was alarming at first when something I enjoyed (a lecture, retreat or sermon) was torn to pieces by my colleagues in the pub afterwards—or, conversely, when something that to me was clearly rubbish seemed to get a good reception. After a while, I realised that 50 per cent of people will hate *anything*. It's kind of reassuring to know that, when you get into the parish, you're doing well if only half the people are slagging you off at any one time.

But what you mostly learn is that people are basically messed up. The Common Life is not about bringing out the best in people. Being 'on best behaviour' is something most folk manage, at best, for a few hours a day, and what sustains it is the other hours when we're allowed to be at our worst. The Common Life is an integrated life, a life without the compartments and boundaries and floodgates that keep the chaos of our inner selves safely quarantined from having consequences in the outside world. It's about being our whole self before God—a self which, it turns out, averages out a lot further from perfection than we like to imagine. Far from bringing out the best, it's more likely to bring to the surface all that is unresolved in us: all our insecurities, all the hidden dysfunction of our relationships, all the questions never asked and the doubts never answered. If you're very, very lucky, it might even give you the chance to deal with some of them. If you are ever going to find yourself in hospital, or marriage guidance, or psychotherapy, this will be the time when it happens.

The result is often not a model of Christian community, but, at the same time, it's a unique and privileged opportunity to share those struggles. When it came to our final tutor group meeting and the person leading the prayers spoke the name of each person present, for every person I could silently add my own prayers for the particular needs and struggles I knew they were facing.

Life in college is like a soap opera—not because everybody gets killed in a plane crash just in time for the Christmas special, but because everything that happens to any one person here happens to the community. It isn't just that I know everybody, but that everybody I am connected to is also connected to everybody else. There's an intensity, a saturation of relationships. Everything that happens is a part of the story of all of us.

The college is like an organism. During the vacations, when the college community was in suspended animation, I felt cut off from my feelings. Left behind in Mirfield when everyone else was away, I was like a bee without a hive, an ant without a hill. When they came back, the stream of my life began to run again.

It is the painful privilege of being 'one body' that you can feel when the community is sick. Mattins is the time to take the temperature; if the college is off-colour, it comes out in the singing. Perhaps the lowest moment of my first year was when I realised during morning prayer that rivalries and insecurities were being played out right there, in our worship. Battles could be won and lost during the Benedictus; alliances could be forged or neutrality preserved with a choice of phrase in the intercessions.

So there are things I won't miss about the intensity of this life. The gossip. The way that a hasty email or ill-judged intercession becomes the equivalent of a tabloid scandal ('bookgate', 'stolegate', 'Mattinsgate'). The simple inability of most people to put up with most other people. If nothing else, it shows you what every church since the time of St Paul is up against—human nature. It has brought home to me how far I fall short of what ought to be expected of any human being, let alone a priest. It would be humbling were it not that everyone else is just as bad. And when you think that it takes the church two or five or ten years to select each of these people... there are times when I wonder if *anybody* out there is functional.

Yet here I have seen for the first (and possibly last) time what it really means to be 'members one of another', rejoicing with those who rejoice and mourning with those who mourn. Here, our lives matter to one another, not because we are friends or we like one another or we have something in common, but simply because we are part of one another, and that not to be interested in one another's welfare would be as inconceivable as not to care for our own. Here perhaps we can begin—only begin—to learn what it means to love others 'as ourselves'.

Getting real

If loving my neighbours was sometimes difficult, loving God was (up to a point) easier than it had ever been.

The first and most obvious thing you notice at the monastery is the change of pace. It is not that people are not busy or that they don't hurry; a monk legging it down the path is a sight to be seen (or, perhaps, avoided, if one is of a delicate disposition: they don't wear trousers under those cassocks). But some things are not allowed to be rushed, and one of those things is prayer. You can tell a visitor in church straight away, because they say the Lord's Prayer like someone coming off a motorway: it takes them a couple of lines to realise they're overtaking everyone else. But within a couple of days, a pace that at first seemed artificially slow reveals itself to be perfectly natural. Elsewhere, we've simply got out of the habit of taking time to actually listen to the words we're saying. After I'd been at college for a term, I went back to morning prayer at the cathedral of my old diocese and just couldn't keep up. It felt like being asked to breathe more quickly.

The words here are slow because they emerge out of silence. Silence is the default; silence underlies everything. At the end of each line, silence is what we go back to. The words are like stitches, the needle dipping in and out, embroidering the music on to a ground of silence. We have choir practice every week and the choir is everyone, musical ability or lack of it notwithstanding. The result was sometimes a bit painful for my cathedral-singer husband! But I think of the music the way I think of the cassock; it isn't there as an embellishment, it's just what we clothe the words in, so that we don't obscure them with our own personal interpretations. They also say that singing together affects people's heartrate and breathing, that you physically become more in sync with one another. And maybe, when we sing the song of the angels, we are bringing earth just a little bit more into harmony with heaven.

There are also longer rhythms that come into play, the rhythms of days and years and seasons. Now, I'm English, so of course I talk about the weather. A former colleague of mine from New Zealand once suggested that the 'Britishness test' for citizenship should be replaced with a single sentence: 'It's snowing', to which the correct answer is 'But it won't stick.' And there certainly is a lot of weather in Yorkshire. I arrived in the middle of a hurricane and briefly wondered if I had let myself in for three years of being unable to walk upright. But it's our round of daily prayer that has really drawn my attention to the turning of the seasons. In winter, we walked to Mattins through darkness and occasional snow, feast days marked by an extra ration of daylight. We would enter in silence and blackness and watch as the windows slowly lightened through our time of worship, and then we were sent out into the new-consecrated day that had been prepared for us while we were praying.

We don't have stained glass, but we have something better. We have each day, a brand-new limited edition work of art by the Almighty's hand—a sunset the colour of seraph's wings, or autumn leaves against a hot blue sky, or the febrile glow of a storm about to break. It is a daily gift, unrepeatable, a direct celebration of the seasons of which our muted echo is the liturgical round of greens, purples and golds. Even the church herself has moods. I am sometimes startled to come in at a different time of day and see the church with a different face.

It's not hard to feel close to God here. On the best days, everything seems to fall out so that, somehow, you will be in the right place at the right time to help someone else or to be helped by them. You can feel that God is at work here and that each of us is at his service, ready to be put to use. Sometimes, after I've spent an hour or so in an art gallery, 'tuning myself in' to created beauty, I am struck by the beauty of something perfectly ordinary and accidental—a wall or a tree or the fortuitous composition of a bucket and spade. Maybe that's what we're doing here. There's a hymn about mission which tells us to seek the presence of God 'in each time and space' ('Go to the world' by Sylvia Dunstan). Well, we spend an hour or more each day looking on God revealed in glory—God recognition exercises, if you like— so that when we step out of church, we can see his signs everywhere.

If I thought that college was all going to be one long retreat, though, I was wrong. I thought I was going to leave behind the shabby old secular me, covered in the dust of the world, and be upgraded to a shiny new spiritual superhero. Two years in, and I felt my prayer life had gone backwards. Nothing had prepared me for the knock my prayer life was going to take when I came to college. I was in church twice or three times a day, and I was praying less.

The problem was, what had been my private prayer was

now public prayer. Before I came to college, I was used to the daily office being my private time with God. Now that had been taken away from me. The prayer that had once hallowed my home and my household had been relocated five minutes down the road to college; home was no longer where my heart was. What I was experiencing is familiar to anyone in public ministry. It sounds like everyone's dream, to get paid for doing what you love, but there's also sacrifice— allowing your private sources of sustenance to become public property. Even when we're praying privately, we're praying in public. Praying in church—actually allowing yourself to pray—is exposing. Anyone who has been on retreat with me (and that means the whole college) knows that I tend to get a bit emotional when I pray. I don't weep like a fairytale princess or a Hollywood heroine, a single tear bejewelling my flawless cheek. I cry like a human gunk machine. I shed those delicate-sounding 'tears of contrition' as if the entire 60 per cent water content of my body is trying to escape through my face. It is not in any way private.

I also had to say goodbye to my old spiritual director. My new one was a wise and holy monk, who had many years' experience at the coalface of prayer, and, for him, prayer was a straightforward matter of just getting on with it. I was slightly in awe, and spent the first year of our meetings turning up at his room like a child visiting a kindly headmaster, to report that indeed I was well, thank you, sir.

In your average parish church (and if there is such a thing as an average church, spiritually speaking, mine was probably it), people don't really talk about their prayer life. It's kind of assumed that people are doing it, in the way that it's assumed married couples are having sex, but, in the same way, you wouldn't start comparing your frequency with someone else's over coffee at the back of church. Nor was there any guidance as to what would be 'normal' or 'healthy' or 'expected'. It's one of the great frustrations of being an Anglican that you can't just look up the rules. In fact, in my confirmation class I remember there being some resistance to the idea that prayer was something that could be learned or practised at all: no 'Lord, teach us to pray' here! So I guessed (with not much to compare myself to) that praying the offices twice a day was probably considered pretty good.

But in college it seemed as if everyone was getting it more than I was. There definitely are expectations here, and praying the offices was about as much of an achievement as getting out of bed. The minimum expected of us was to put aside 20 minutes each day for private prayer—preferably the same 20 minutes. Simple, yes? Well, sure, although you might need a computer algorithm to identify a suitable daily slot, given that your timetable for every day will be completely different. And who manages to switch prayer on and off at 20-minute intervals, anyway?

Everyone except me, apparently.

One of the hardest things about community living is the comparisons. Of course you can't really know what's going on between someone else and God; God keeps his confidences. But the point of living together is to learn from each other—to observe, and to work out how things are done in this community—so it shouldn't be surprising if we end up judging our spiritual lives in the same way.

One of the things many people do during the discernment or formation process is to have a personality type test. What mine showed was that (in layman's terms) I am loud, absent-minded, over-intellectual, impatient and a control freak. Until I took the test, I was rather sceptical of personality typing. When I saw the results, I knew they'd got me bang to rights. Unfortunately, most of the time it seems as if being a 'spiritual person' means being exactly the opposite kind of person from me. I lose track of the times I hear it casually mentioned that priests tend to be introverts, or that we're mostly introverts here. I even found out that my personality type is the one least likely to be found in a monastery. After all, prayer (it sometimes seemed to me) is basically sitting down and shutting up. That made me pretty much a lost cause.

It has taken me most of my time at college to give up trying to make my prayer life fit somebody else's preconceived notion of what spirituality ought to look like. Maybe other people can create silence for themselves just by turning off the noise. I can't. I can only find it, sometimes, like Elijah did in 1 Kings 19—through the earthquake, wind and fire. I was delighted when a Romanian nun told me, 'We don't really have that concept of sitting in silence.' Orthodox monasticism seems to be doing pretty well for a bunch of people who have allegedly never mastered their '20 minutes a day'.

Maybe it's OK not to be a spiritual superhero straight away. I have one friend at college who used to live in Italy and can no longer share our appreciation for pub lasagne and Co-op salad-in-a-bag. Well, I guess in the same way you can become a prayer gourmet too. This is, after all, a monastery, so prayer is the speciality *della casa*. In my case, there's the added difficulty of my tendency to leap straight into the most difficult stage of anything. The first time we were told to choose our own recipes for a school cookery class (I would have been eleven or twelve, and could barely manage a Pot Noodle), I decided to make homemade tortelloni. (I blame my parents: when my father decided he wanted to learn the organ, he started with Bach's Toccata and Fugue in D minor.) But I think where I've got to right now is that there's nothing wrong with the basics: asking God for what I need, thanking him for what he gives me, and trying to turn away from sin and cling closer to Christ. God actually wants to give us good things. Who, when a child asks for a fish, would give him a snake? Sometimes I feel we're the ones asking for snakes!

In the end, what I've learned here is what is real. We often hear the world outside described as 'the real world' or 'real life'. We sometimes fall into it ourselves. But the truth, the truth that doesn't get talked about much in the 'real world', even in churches, is the glory of God, the kingship of Christ, the victory of the cross. That's what I had managed to miss, back in that not-quite-so-real world. We hear Bible readings week after week about judgement and joy, plan and prophecy, cosmic battle and second coming, and we come home having learned that Jesus was a good chap and we should all be nice to one another.

For instance, a few years ago, I would have been dismissive of any talk about angels and demons or fighting the powers of evil—dismissive in a keep-smiling-and-walk-away-quickly kind of way. But something like pursuing a vocation to the priesthood is kind of… conspicuous. And in a monastery! If you're going to live in a spiritual armaments factory, you need to wise up quickly. Let's just say, this is a place where people can stand around the bar and talk about spiritual warfare and nobody thinks it's a joke. And angels? I've not met one personally, but I can believe I'm within six degrees of separation.

Here in college there's a chance, just a chance, that we can start to talk about our faith as if it's for real. In the monastery church, in one of the chapels, there is a large icon of the resurrection—the way it's usually depicted in the Eastern Church, as Christ trampling down the powers of death—and the background is golden. Sometimes, when God's wisdom and atmospheric refraction have done a particularly spectacular job of the sunset, I look at the sky and remember that the icon is a window on to reality. The background of our lives is uncreated light, teeming with angels. And the sky is golden.

In the spotlight

They say that life is not a dress rehearsal. At college, you'd be forgiven for thinking that's exactly what it is. There's always a rehearsal to go to, and quite often a bit of dressing-up, too. Specifically, we spend a lot of time rehearsing the liturgy. Mostly, though, we don't rehearse the liturgy we will ultimately be carrying out; we do not have practical exams where we have to perform all seven sacraments in under two hours; nor do we get to roleplay bridezillas or grieving relatives. We spend most of our rehearsal time on parts we will never have to play again after we leave, such as acolyte. (Acolyte comes from the word for 'to follow', because it mostly involves following somebody who looks as if they know where they're going, but made a teensy bit more perilous by holding a big candle quite near to your hair.) More generally, though, what we're rehearsing for is a new role—a new part to play in a divine drama with a 2000-year run and counting.

I've been on stage (not counting the leading role in my primary school production of *Wind in the Willows*) twice in my life. I've sung Gilbert and Sullivan in a grass skirt and bikini top, so standing in front of a congregation in nothing but a cassock doesn't feel quite so exposed. Once you get backstage, there is nothing glamorous about show business. Up close, the lavish velvet and organza of the princess's train is really nasty silver tinsel. That daring directorial decision the critics got exercised about? It was just someone in the lighting box who couldn't read their own handwriting. I once got the chance to serve as acolyte at the shrine of Our Lady of Walsingham, and the bit of lacy stuff under the six big candlesticks was a wipe-clean plastic tablecloth. Liturgy is not show business, not really, but they both have a backstage.

Priesthood is often described as a 'role'. We mean that it's not a job—although priests certainly do jobs. It doesn't, or shouldn't, mean that priesthood is an act, but it is nevertheless about playing a certain part, about embodying a certain character in a convincing way. And like a performance, nine-tenths of it is in the preparation. The other tenth is in whether or not you panic when the preparation lets you down.

Liturgy at college runs like clockwork. At 7.25 every morning, the lights in the chapel go on, and out from the sacristy wheels a little ordinand, like a figurine on an antique clock. This person is the day's Officiant.

The dignity and gravity of this role is enhanced by the wearing of a surplice. A fully fledged surplice makes even the slimmest ordinand look like a small yurt. I am not the slimmest ordinand, and I look like a scale model of Mont Blanc. Of course, Full English is not the only option. There is the Continental variation, the cotta, worn by Romans and those of Roman sympathies—a crisply pleated, cropped number, often indecently short and sometimes adorned with lace. I am told that surplices are tax deductible for clergy, as a requisite of their work. Cottas, being more in the manner of a private fetish, are not.

The first time I led Mattins, fresh from a job with plenty of public speaking, I sailed through it—appropriately enough, since I was rigged out in enough cloth to furnish a decent-sized schooner. Another year at the college, and I have mastered the appropriate air of abject terror. You remember what it's like when you have an exam? The way you start to panic that your three alarm clocks will all fail? That you'll somehow forget it's happening (in spite of being up all night worrying about it) and accidentally spend the morning in front of the TV instead? Or maybe that you'll disqualify yourself by compulsively jumping up from your desk and shouting? Yeah. Like that.

Mattins is, in fact, a lot like an exam; once you're in there, you're on your own. Ideally, proper execution of the duties of the Officiant requires a tuning fork, a precision Swiss chronometer with a radio link to the atomic clock, and a prescription for valium. Failing that, I have found you can get by with an old phone with menus in Cyrillic, an accomplice in the congregation, and an ability to look as if you know what you're doing. In other words, what I've learned is both preparation (what other people might call 'paranoia') and liturgical instinct (what other people might call 'winging it').

You see, the point is not just to become good at doing the liturgy in one particular way, which you will never have to do again. That would be a bit like the way my driving instructor taught me to parallel park by lining up certain parts of the car. I can now do perfect manoeuvres *so long as the car is a dual-control diesel Citroen C3*. No, the point is to hone your 'liturgical instinct'. Mirfield liturgy, you could say, is a bit like fencing. It is precise; it is rarefied; it involves wearing white and carrying dangerous objects. It doesn't much resemble what's going to happen when somebody jumps out of a dark alley with something sharp, but ultimately what you do in that situation is determined by what you did in rehearsal.

We got a chance to test out our nascent liturgical instincts a few weeks into the course, when we were sent out to parishes. In the parish, there is no such thing as preparation. Advance warning means knowing whether you're the crucifer or the deacon *before* the advertised start time for the service. But strangely enough, those weeks of doing it right had given us the confidence to take the lead when we were needed. A week into our placement, a locum priest turned to my fellow student and me and asked for help because 'on my course they didn't teach liturgy'. We had been at college about six weeks at this point, but such is the reputation of Mirfield.

Being thrown in at the deep end is not my favourite way of learning, but it does give you experiences you'd never get in class. I have mimed all the hymns in a service because I couldn't turn my radio mic off. I have climbed on to a church roof armed with a watering can on a fishing rod (wearing a cassock, of course). I have spent half an hour with my arms down a heating grid while trying to keep the dust off my lacy cotta. You put on that cassock, and suddenly you're supposed to be the one who knows how to fix problems.

But there's more to public ministry than knowing how to keep your cool. Liturgy rehearsal is also about being a liturgical person. Serving in the sanctuary is a spiritual discipline, a humbling of oneself under the liturgy. They may be 'on show', but the best servers are completely inconspicuous. No flashy trainers, no hair bows, no showy cornering during the procession: just a white robe named Acolyte No 1. And every action during the liturgy is a liturgical action, so when a server moves, they move liturgically. There's an apocryphal story about a server who once had to put out a fire in the sanctuary—but didn't forget to bow to the altar first. The liturgy may not always run as smoothly as clockwork, but we aim to be like the hands of a clock, moving silently and always pointing away from ourselves.

The idea is that this mindful, liturgical movement will spread out into the rest of our lives—that we will, in the words of St Benedict, handle the pots and pans in the kitchen as if we were handling the sacred vessels. I don't think I've remembered to do that once yet (unless operating an industrial dishwasher in a cassock counts), but the training certainly shows. Our 'signature' at Mirfield is the Mirfield Hands—always clasped in front. When I went on placement to a charismatic church, everybody was swaying and dancing, and I was joining in enthusiastically... from the waist down. My arms were going nowhere. Mirfield Hands!

Liturgy isn't the only behind-the-scenes experience we get. One of the most interesting glimpses into what our future role might involve was the cheerily named Death and Dying Week. On our tour of the crem, we were introduced to the little button that we will one day have to press, and even got a glimpse into the ovens. The 'boxes' ('we don't call them bodies') take about 90 minutes to burn, we were told, as long as they have a good amount of body fat. And I can confirm that they really do put the right person's ashes in the urn. I've seen where they do it. As our guide said, cheerfully, 'Just be careful of your clothes, it's dusty in here.' (Strictly speaking, most household dust is dead skin cells, and we're all made of stardust, or whatever it is they say. What goes around comes around. So I probably have bits of dead people in my hair, like, all the time... I can't say this thought reassured me one bit.)

It seems that one of the things people still associate the clergy with is death. Even the funeral parlour was decorated with what can only be described as a religious theme. If you want to convey 'mortality', without anything as in-your-face as skulls and worms, then Christianity is your tasteful option. And I was surprised to find that coffins actually do look like coffins—lozenge shaped, as in vampire movies and Goth jewellery. I thought it was a bit, well, *morbid*, but apparently people like to have what they've seen on telly. I was also surprised to hear about the way the undertakers match the families up with 'a clergy'. Denomination and parish are irrelevant, but they still want to have one. Apparently, we are a necessary accessory in the décor of death. Just make sure you look like one off the telly.

For all these new experiences, I was missing one thing from the time before I came to college—my ministry. I was preparing for a life in public ministry but, ironically, public ministry was the one thing I wasn't doing. My workplace, although it had nothing to do with religion, had been my daily chance to live out my Christian values in a way that was visible to others. Even more artificial was being no longer a member of any parish church. After only a few years as a layperson, I had said a permanent goodbye to the pews. The next time I went back into a parish church, several weeks after starting college, I was going not as a parishioner but as a student on placement; the church was not my spiritual family but a 'ministry context'. I had become an ecclesiastical anthropologist: 'church' and 'world' alike were foreign cultures to be observed rather than lived in.

In fact, the main thing I seemed to be learning on placement was that people in church lose all sense of normal and acceptable behaviour. In one church, my first contact with 'normal parishioners' was an elbow plonked on my shoulder, shortly followed by the owner of said elbow leaning right across me to introduce himself to my (male) fellow ordinand. I don't generally invite people to treat my upper body as a mantelpiece, at least not before we've been introduced, but I didn't think that stepping sharply sideways and letting him fall on the floor would be a great start, especially since he was introducing himself as the Sunday school teacher. Another chap gave us a cheery rundown of the faults and failings of his fellow parishioners and apologised for the absence of one on sick leave because—here he illustrated with rather graphic hand actions in front of his chest—'she's had the full chop'.

My colleague and I had a good laugh about how unbelievable it was, but this was our life from now on. We'd opted for following the truth, and the truth is that people are pretty crazy.

After a few weeks 'in the field', we got together to reflect. The experience of most of my fellow students was that they were automatically treated as clergy, but I found myself almost envious of other people's tricky pastoral conversations. Congregations of older ladies just didn't look at me and think 'future priest'. They thought 'reminds me of my granddaughter'. On my first day in placement, one woman said straight out that I looked too young. Another asked why I didn't wear lippy and nail varnish and generally make more of myself. (I was tempted to point out that there were several old gentlemen in the congregation, and I didn't want to subject them to too much excitement at their time of life.) It seemed I was never going to be mistaken for a priest: on the contrary, on my first day in one place, the archdeacon was mistaken for me. Maybe people's expectations of the age and experience of a theological student are a bit on the high side. Of course, everyone was very supportive to the nice young girl on placement, anxious to look after me and offer me lifts and wish me good luck for my 'first' sermon—even though I'd been doing it for two years. I was supposed to be ministering to them, and they wouldn't stop ministering to me...

It was only during my first summer that I finally got a taste of truly public ministry. I'd been told to turn up, in inner-city London, in my cassock. I was used to it at home or in church; this was the first time I'd worn it on public transport.

The cassock is a controversial garment. In the church, there is a whole subtle (and sometimes less than subtle) grammar of clerical dress by which clergy can send out coded signals to position themselves in relation to one another, like members of some underworld gang or perhaps an advanced species of pack animal. Millimetres of collar and inches of sock can denote precise degrees of elevation up the liturgical 'candle'. A patterned shirt or a pair of heels can be subversive. Even when everybody is wearing the same cassock twice a day, somehow it can become a political statement. In London, it's an instrument for urban mission in the 21st century.

This being London, of course, where the existence of other people is not to be acknowledged at any cost, most people didn't bat an eyelid. They just assumed it was one of the thousand-and-one things going on in that huge crazy city which was completely alien for them but completely normal for somebody else. In fact, one morning as I was sitting having a coffee in London Bridge station, a pair of small tanned male hands appeared over my glasses. 'This is London,' I thought. 'This is probably normal. In a few seconds I will find out why this is perfectly normal...' It was followed a few moments later by the sight of a rather sweet and embarrassed young man who had mistaken me for his girlfriend. Yup: full-length binbag and bottle-blonde hair, like a nun having a crisis, but in London I just look like some guy's girlfriend.

The cassock starts conversations. Sometimes it's 'Are you a vicar?' or (depending on hat) 'Are you a rabbi?' I got the occasional 'What's that?' and even one 'What are you wearing underneath?' One woman I met in a textile art exhibition complimented me on my radical fashion statement. But it's amazing how many people are just looking for a way in to start talking to a priest. It led to plenty of impromptu ministry, from listening to the bereaved friend of a suicide victim to saying evening prayer on a train with a methadone addict. If you think Londoners don't want to talk to strangers, just try wearing a cassock. I realised, in a way that I hadn't before, that every kind of clothing is about status and statement. A priest in a suit is saying something about their class and about how they see their priestly role in relation to secular professions. A priest in a cassock is trying, at least as far as possible, to step outside that perception. Of course, there are going to be people who respond negatively, but even that is the start of a conversation. Most uniforms are there to hide behind, to make us safer. This one is to make us more vulnerable.

My placements also gave me a perspective on what actually matters in a church. After a few weeks in my first placement, I thought college liturgy had spoiled me for ever. How could I pray with that random assortment of crumpled linen all over the altar? How could I process in with dignity

113

when I had to swerve round that chair? How could I love my neighbours with the churchwarden shouting spelling corrections for the notice sheet from the back of the church? (It made me wish I could quote the law against 'interrupting a minister in the course of divine service'.) Yet this was a 'good' church; it had solid attendance figures and no obvious dysfunction. Any problem I had was surely mine.

To my surprise, though, in my visits to various churches, I found it wasn't liturgy or good order that ultimately mattered to me. Some of the most spiritually profound services I attended were complete chaos. Don't get me wrong; I've always been a liturgical snob, and now I'm a liturgical snob with theological qualifications to back me up. But in the end I'd rather be in a congregation where people feel able to wave their hands during the songs and to kiss strangers (me!) than one where they pride themselves on always winning the Mrs Sunderland Bible Reading Contest. Not because I don't admire the latter, but because I have nothing to offer them. Some churches know they're a 'good' church (like people say a 'good' school) and don't need to worry, and everybody is fine without you, thank you very much. But in places where life is a little bit tougher, a little bit more precarious, you find moments of raw openness to the gospel. In the end, if you want to know whether the Spirit has or has not left the building, it comes down to the people, and when people are open to receiving me and what little I might have to offer, that is something for which I am profoundly grateful.

The female of the species

Before I joined the church, the fact that I'm female was just that—a fact. I know there are people who go around with something called a gender identity; if I have such a thing, I've never yet bothered to locate it. For me, being female just means I have a female body and I've grown up with the social expectations that apply to girls. It's just the situation I find myself in. Sure, there are differences between boys and girls that aren't just about private parts but, as it happens, I'm no good at either multitasking or spatial awareness, so I have the worst of both worlds. I'm a woman in the same way I'm English: I've turned out this way because this was where I grew up, but it could very well have been otherwise.

It's only been since becoming a Christian that this circumstance—my being a woman—has been something I've had to consciously think about. Feminist friends will probably deplore my lack of awareness, but I can honestly say I don't remember ever feeling that I had experienced sexism, and certainly not from guys my own age with more than two brain cells to rub together. Even my supervisor back in my university days, who was rumoured to be the original inspiration for the character of Uncle Monty in *Withnail and I*, and whose misogyny was legendary, managed to overlook my gender so far as to favour me with excellent tea and cake in supervision sessions by the time my dissertation was finished.

But pretty much as soon as I entered church circles, I became aware that I was A Woman, not just a person who coincidentally happened to have a bosom. The church isn't sexist in a nasty way, exactly; it isn't (usually) misogynistic. It's sexist in a nice way, which I sometimes think is worse. Church sexism means always being asked what your husband does. It's the assumption that you will want to help out with the children's group. It's ladies in the congregation taking food round for single male priests because they assume that only women can cook for themselves. It's the culture in which female clergy on official lists (BAP panels, diocesan registers and so forth) mention their husband's work and their children rather than their qualifications and experience. In the church, it seems, it's not possible to say anything about a woman without mentioning her husband. When a senior clergywoman came to speak at the college, all I knew about her was her name, her role, and the fact that her husband was a priest. It isn't *intended* to make a woman feel like an adjunct to her husband. It's just a hangover of the Church of England's village green mentality, where everybody is somebody else's spouse or sister or cousin. Whatever your husband does or doesn't do, a few domestic details make everyone feel more comfortable.

As soon as I mention what I'm doing with my life, the conversation turns to gender. I say, 'I'm training to be a priest' and I might as well have said, '... and I'm a woman, you know!' As I've said, non-church people generally ask if I'm going to be a bishop or, occasionally, if I'm going to be the Vicar of Dibley. Perhaps, only my becoming a fictional character is less likely than my becoming a bishop. That's unless the whole issue has passed them by, of course, in which case they look confused and ask if women can do that. Church people ask, 'So is your husband a priest?' I seem to be a particular novelty for evangelicals. A friend once invited me to dinner along with another friend of theirs, a committed evangelical Christian, presumably (and not unreasonably) reckoning we'd have a lot in common. My fellow guest looked thoughtful for a while and finally told me she could accept female clergy but couldn't imagine them being married. It's a good thing theological argument is my idea of a great night. I'm not so sure my friends agreed, though.

It's only going to get worse, because one day, God and the bishop willing, I will not be just a woman but a 'woman priest'. That's a term I try to avoid whenever possible. I prefer 'female priest'; at least it sounds less as if I'm going to become some kind of hybrid creature. I don't think that male priesthood and female priesthood are two different categories. When I am ordained, I will enter into the same diaconate and the same priesthood as my male colleagues. It's just that I will be me-being-a-priest and hence a woman being a priest. A fellow student was recently asked to consider 'how she was going stand behind the altar as a woman'. Her answer, very sensibly, was that she could hardly stand behind it as anything else.

However, the interaction between the role or social image of 'woman' and the role of 'priest' is different from that between 'man' and 'priest'. 'Priest' is a paradoxical category, historically speaking—both high status and, at the same time, humbling. I once knew a (male) priest who made a great virtue at public events out of doing the washing-up. He clearly thought it demonstrated his humility. A female friend remarked that he ought to just get a dishwasher. For me, that illustrated something crucial about the very different challenges that men and women face in the priestly role. A male priest with his cassock-sleeves rolled up, elbow-deep in sudsy water, is an image of refreshing humility, of authority overturned. A woman in the same picture is just a woman. The same priest once advised a newly ordained female colleague to get into the kitchen with the other ladies and help prepare sandwiches. Apparently, this was meant as genuine advice on bonding with the parishioners, and he was sincerely amazed when she was offended. I was not.

Most of the time, I find all this slightly amusing. I recognise that some women wouldn't; perhaps it's my innate arrogance, but, if somebody is unintentionally sexist toward me, I generally think the joke is on them. But when it's at the institutional level, then it's serious. At my BAP, I was asked (over the meal table, which seemed a little inappropriate for a question challenging the whole basis of my application) whether, as a married woman, I was truly 'deployable' as required of stipendiary clergy. In other words, would a husband really be prepared to give up his job to follow his wife?

The fact that my husband did move, and that I was prepared to ask him to, seems to put us in a minority. Women now make up 50 per cent of new clergy, but, among those being trained residentially for stipendiary ministry (the ones the church is investing most in), it's a much lower proportion. It used to be worse. In the early years of women's ordination, many dioceses would give married clergy couples only one or one-and-a-half stipends for two full-time posts. Perhaps their reasoning—lifted from that of Victorian factory owners—was that a woman's income is only ever a 'supplement' to the household budget. Maternity leave was non-existent. Anybody who thinks women's ordination was some kind of feminist victory needs to think again. The only 'right' those women won was the 'right' to work for nothing.

Mirfield has been a mixed-sex college for several years. In a student body that changes completely every two to three years, that's basically for ever, but reputations take rather longer to change, especially in the church. I've been to parties where the ecclesiastical gossip being avidly picked over at the dinner table dated from 20 years before. So people are often surprised that I'm able to be here at all, let alone that I would want to be. They don't ask, 'What's it like being at Mirfield?' but, 'What's it like *being a woman* at Mirfield?' Even though I know what they mean, it still makes me laugh. I'm a woman wherever I am; I don't know what it would be like to be anything else.

Well, I can now exclusively reveal what it's like to be this particular woman at Mirfield. To begin with, it was no big deal. As it happened, I was the only woman in my class. There were four women in total but, with different years and courses, my classes ended up being just me and nine blokes. I don't know what this says about me, but it took quite some weeks for this fact even to register in my mind. As far as I was concerned, I was just one of the guys.

Personally, I don't mind being kind-of mistaken for a man. A very conservative friend of mine expressed horror when I mentioned a potential curacy post with a female priest as supervisor: '"She"?? Oh… you're a "she", too!' There are advantages to being an honorary chap—such as being able to drink beer, smoke a pipe and be very rude to one's closest friends while still somehow having the novelty value and privileges of being the girl—although it must be said that there can be boundary issues. Just because a girl thinks she's one of the guys, it doesn't mean the guys are necessarily oblivious to the physiological differences.

Nevertheless, while I might take 'honorary bloke' as a compliment, it was more a source of anxiety for some of my female colleagues. There is a loss of individual expression involved in priestly formation, but does that also mean a loss of femininity? Does neutral mean de facto male? Some of us were happy to wear our cassocks and regulation flat black shoes: it can be a liberation in a world that judges women on their clothes. For others, though, heels and dangly earrings were a necessity, a way of protecting some shred of their personal identity from being subsumed in an alien and masculine world. It still shocks me that female clergy who wear dresses—sensible knee-length pencil skirts with clerical collars—may be considered inappropriately sexy when the same clothes in the office would be thought perfectly professional. Most people have got their heads around the idea that women can be priests, but they haven't quite grasped that priests can be women.

It wasn't only the women who found themselves exploring issues of gender expression in the context of formation. Priesthood is not the most typically macho of life choices, and it doesn't always attract the most typically macho guys—although I dare you to say that to some of the former wrestlers and military men at the college. The most blokey bloke can be caught off guard when his kid asks why daddy is wearing 'a dress'.

Later on in my time at college, the ratio of men to women reached 50–50. Suddenly, the place was full of nail polish and fabulous tights (and, indeed, fabulous legs). My brief respite from the pressures of womanhood was over. There was even a dieting club. Delighted as I am that the college has shaken off its female-unfriendly reputation, and I certainly enjoy shattering people's preconceptions, nothing makes a woman feel inferior like someone who does the being-a-woman thing better. Nevertheless, it seems pretty clear that diversity has injected a little sanity. My direct experience of all-male groups is, of course, non-existent, but I've seen what homogeneity and 'feeling safe' can do—how dangerously easy it is for the outrageous to become acceptable. I enjoy gin, lace and backbiting as much as the next man, but when we say we're forming 'priestly character', I don't think Frankie-Boyle-meets-Dame-Edna-Everage is quite the character we're after.

There was only one time when I felt out of place 'being a woman' at college. A few months after I arrived, the college held a festival to celebrate the transformation of the church building, and all the old boys were invited. And they mostly were boys, or, rather, old men. Only a handful of women were present. I wasn't prepared for the reaction of some of the men to seeing female students in their old college—namely, delight! Several older priests came and congratulated me, as if having two X-chromosomes were some kind of personal achievement. But the big shock was when I went to the loos and saw that someone had stuck a 'Gents' sign over the 'Ladies' sign. Of course, it was mere practicality, a simple case of supply and demand. Nevertheless, it somehow felt like a slap: there are no women here; you don't exist. That was my brief insight into the experience that my older female colleagues had faced. Maybe 'being a woman at Mirfield' is a big deal after all.

— ✳ —

My time at college also coincided with the series of votes and debates on the consecration of women to the episcopate, including the shock defeat for the first measure, which made national news for several days. I tried not to follow events too closely; I've never been able to watch horror films without covering my eyes, and, with friends on both sides, it was always going to be gory. As the day of the vote approached, I saw some subtle changes on friends' Facebook pages—croziers appearing on some, purple ribbons on others—but the debate was getting more visible attention in the world outside than here in college.

Unfortunately, as a female ordinand, I'm taking sides simply by existing. I said the church wasn't sexist in a nasty way, and mostly that's true. Even in the most catholic circles, I've usually been pleasantly surprised. I've worn a cotta at Walsingham and a cassock at the Society of Mary's October Devotions (translation for normal folk: conventions for Virgin Mary fanboys), but it is hard not to be a little resentful of your male colleagues when you're struggling to make ends meet and you realise that some of them are getting money from Anglo-Catholic charitable funds pretty much just for being male. You also know that you won't be judged just as yourself; you are a representative of the entire female half of the species. A man in bad vestments is just a man with bad taste, but when a woman wears a stole that makes you want to wash your eyeballs in acid, it's due to the deficiency of her sex—and she's probably an evangelical or a liberal, or possibly both, just for good measure. I don't particularly covet the 'catholic' label myself, but it's still galling when I see it applied to any bloke who owns a black clerical shirt, while a woman would practically need papal endorsement. A male priest who sings like an air-raid siren is endearing; a woman who sounds a little 'shrill' or 'shrieky' (how gendered are those words?!) is clear evidence of divine disapproval.

It's not just those who are opposed to the ordination of women who treat me as some sort of representative of my kind. After the synod defeat, I was bemused to find people coming up to me to apologise or to assure me of their whole-hearted support for women's ordination. Suddenly, I was a representative of women with priestly vocations, and they were shamefaced representatives of the church that had let us down. On my first visit to one placement church, a woman from the PCC cornered me to tell me that men make much worse priests than women. Several dioceses, including the one in which the college is located, put on what could only be described as Commiseration Masses. The one I went to was billed as a celebration of women's ministry, with the strapline 'Called to be bishops, priests and deacons in God's church'. I'm glad to say, though, that references to *l'affaire du synode* were limited to some awkwardly overspecific inter-cessions and a cordial question-and-answer session with the bishop, during which he delicately referred to the subject as 'last November'.

In all this, however, I found myself quite often defending, or at least explaining, the position of my opponents. The way the debate was presented in the press was mostly unrec-ognisable to the people to whom it directly mattered. The coverage was supposedly pro-women, but it was frustrating to see people thinking they were defending 'my' cause when they talked about equal rights and employment opportuni-ties. It was as if everyone had forgotten that female clergy are Christians as well as women. How can you support priests by attacking the church? It was all a bit Jeremy Kyle—a painful family dispute being played out in front of a national audience—and, like any good sibling, *I* wanted to be the one to beat up my brothers, not let anybody else do it.

It was only while I was abroad, studying the Orthodox Church, that I really came to understand the vital significance of ordination in both genders, and what is at risk if we do not affirm it. In the gender-segregated space of the Romanian Orthodox church, I felt for the first time the solidarity of sisterhood among Christian women. There I saw nuns kneeling in the church porch because they were forbidden from entering during their time of the month, and a little girl standing outside the iconostasis while her brother was allowed into the altar area. God was not too proud to accept the hospitality of the virgin's womb, yet, on account of her womb, the church did not extend that intimate hospitality to his little virgin handmaiden.

I realised there that the question of ordained women cannot, in the end, be isolated from the question of women's role in the church and in God's world. Many of my friends would like to hold the position that women are entirely equal in all respects—in capacity, in humanity, in grace—except with regard to the sacramental priesthood. These 'traditionalists' might be surprised to learn that their position is something of a modern novelty. I have come to the conclusion that the arguments supporting the all-male priesthood cannot be chemically extracted from the context that gave them birth—from an anthropology that makes women less holy, less Christian, or even less human than men. Womanhood excluded from the altar is not unrelated to womanhood crouching in the porch.

It was also in Romania that I saw the procession of icons

for the Triumph of Orthodoxy. In Orthodox understanding, the icon is the safeguard of the incarnation: we assert our belief in the full humanity of Christ by depicting him in image. I have come to believe that female ordination is also a necessary safeguard in our time against falling away from the truth we have in Christ—against a less-than-fully-human Christ who has taken on only half our human nature, against a reduction of sacramentality to mere resemblance, against once more making unclean that which God has made clean.

Part 3

Ordinand on the run

There comes a time in any ordinand's training when they just want to run away.

At first I didn't have time for exhaustion or regrets. I was so immersed in my new life in college that I didn't want a life outside or even notice its absence. The starts were early and the schedules intense, but that was almost a novelty after my flexi-time office life. It felt a privilege to have only one day off, like proper grown-up clergy. Busyness has its own temptations, which the best writers on ministry warn against—the perverse sense of status that comes with saying, 'Sorry, I can't; I've got too much on.' For about a year or a bit more, I was living on nervous energy, still pumped up with the excitement of having got there in the first place, but by the middle of the second year, that fuel was running low. The same constraints that had seemed so romantic to a wide-eyed first year—the monastic discipline, the Benedictine virtue of obedience—for a jaded second-year were now starting to chafe.

It wasn't the lack of time so much as the lack of freedom. Unlike 'grown-up' clergy, we couldn't arrange things so as to get off early the night before and spend our Saturday with friends elsewhere in the country. We couldn't say evening prayer privately and get into town for a concert, or decide that, just this once, a family commitment might be more important than a lecture. And yet, put like that, the gripes sounded a bit pathetic—self-indulgent, even. After all, wasn't the ordained life supposed to be a sacrificial life, a costly life, a life of self-giving? That was what we were constantly being told. If ever anyone dared to say they'd like to spend more time with their loved ones, somebody else was bound to bring up that word 'sacrifice', usually in conjunction with 'in the parish...'. Those were the words you couldn't argue with: if you couldn't cope with the little inconveniences of college life, how would you cope with life in the parish? This would be followed by the 'someone dying' scenario. It was all very well wanting to spend time at your child's school or your mother's hospital bedside, the argument went, but what if there was a phone call from someone who was dying? The church has to be available 24/7, and, in practice, that often means the *priest* has to be available—or feeling guilty about not being available.

Missing the 30th birthdays of all my friends, though, didn't feel like a sacrifice I'd made for Christ. It felt like neglecting my responsibilities as a friend. Once or twice I was on the receiving end, plans with clergy friends being dropped at the last minute because of 'a pastoral situation'—as if, because I was a friend, I didn't also have pastoral needs. When I had to tell friends, family or my husband that I was putting college commitments first, I didn't know if that was self-sacrifice or just selfishness. It certainly felt less like the action of a responsible adult, accountable to God and to others for my use of time, and more like a boarding-school girl observing an arbitrary curfew.

The sacrifices of full-time ministry are far more than late nights and missed parties. In one of our lectures, we heard from a female priest who always answered the phone at

2.00 in the morning because it just might be (you guessed it) someone who was dying, even though she knew it would nearly always be sexual harassment from a group of local teenage boys. One of my placement supervisors had been stalked; another priest friend had CCTV installed in his house after being assaulted and robbed, and a photo in the college library commemorated a former student who had made the ultimate sacrifice—died in service, murdered by an ex-con he was trying to help. As one friend memorably commented in class, 'In the Christian life, martyrdom is always an option.' Those things you've always considered non-negotiable priorities—your family, your home, your sanity and safety, all the normal human well-being and dignity that you would want to protect for every other person—all that becomes optional. Just as the Common Life is a life without boundaries, without safety barriers, so is the life of the priest.

What if I couldn't do that? I knew I owed Christ everything, even my life, but I also knew my limits, and God has no use for another burned-out priest. It felt like an impossible choice: burn out or cop out.

It wasn't so much that I didn't know if I was cut out to be a priest. I doubted whether I was cut out to be a Christian at all. On bad days, I wasn't even sure I was up to being human.

In the moment of my conversion, I experienced the good news as a liberation—good news not just for the world, objectively, but also subjectively, for me. It was what inspired me to share the gospel with others. I had absolute confidence that it really was good for a person to come to Christ, good for them and good for the world.

That liberation is still a reality in my life. I could not have imagined being this person or living the life I have now without the encounter that changed everything. In Christ, we have been led out from the bondage of sin and death, from our own addiction to self-destruction. We are a post-Passover people. And yet, it no longer surprises me that Paul—who had his own transforming encounter, with a light so bright that he walked by the remembered brightness of it for the rest of his life—described the Christian life so often in terms of patience, of endurance, of athletic discipline.

Athletic discipline is not something I'm good at. In my second year at college, in terror of my impending 30s, I briefly took up physical exercise. This involved walking only slightly faster than usual but while wearing sporty clothes, which meant it officially counted as exercise. For several years, my excuse for not getting involved in sporting activities had been that I hadn't bought a pair of trainers since I was 15. I also found I had rather more need for a sports bra than when I was 15. But online shopping gave me the courage to venture back into the world of sportswear (is it actually a prerequisite for doing sports to think that purple and lime green look good together?) and thence on to the sports field.

There are a lot of similarities between the Christian life and exercise. Many people say they're members of a gym but never actually turn up. A lot of the people who exercise are fat. In fact, if you just looked at the people in your local gym, you might think that exercise makes you fat. People who exercise a lot say that exercise makes them feel happier, healthier and better all round. Those who don't exercise say that exercise is for masochists who want to make them feel pain and take away their chocolate. It often involves silly clothes, and most of the time it just feels like a lot of hard work that isn't making any difference. St Paul was spot-on when he said that the Christian life is like exercise. I'm not very good at sticking to either of them.

Of course, Paul also talks about joy. It's a funny word, 'joy'. It's the word that appears in embossed gold calligraphy on the front of a Christmas card, while inside what we actually wish for our loved ones is a 'happy' or 'merry' Christmas. Why do we need the word 'joy' when we already have the word 'happiness'? Perhaps because we need a word to mean a special Christian kind of happiness that doesn't actually make you feel happy. Joy is that which can be seen over the course of a year or a lifetime but doesn't necessarily seem to involve enjoying many of the minutes.

Joy, spiritual joy, the joy of the Christian life, is an acquired taste, and I'd had 25 years of atheist life in which to acquire precisely the opposite tastes. My emotional taste buds, if you like, were calibrated to the flesh rather than the spirit. I started to think that maybe I was terminally programmed to follow too much the devices and desires of my own heart. I was that aberration of late modernity, the Individual.

To explain the last comment, I must first introduce you to the Principal (or, rather, reacquaint you, since the monk who interviewed me on my first visit to the college had, since then, been named as Principal)—a man of enormous intellect, attired in a paint-splattered monastic cassock and preaching from an incongruous smartphone.

Where most preachers would start with an amusing anecdote about their childhood misdemeanours or a funny incident on the bus last Tuesday-week, and move with a Godwards swerve (more or less graceful, depending on the skill of the preacher) on to the gospel of the day, Father Principal would preach on the novels of Charles Williams or an incident from Winnie the Pooh. Once, he answered a question about Plato (if I remember correctly) by reference to Paddington Bear, as if the connection were perfectly obvious. His utterances were elusive and allusive, full with a volume of meaning only dimly perceived by the hearers and often preceded by a thoughtful inward gaze, as if he were grasping to translate into the language of mortals what he perceived therein.

One of Father's favourite phrases was 'the conditions of late modernity'. In moments of idle speculation, I wondered whether, after modernity and late modernity and post-modernity, we would fall off the edge of time altogether, for lack of any terminology to go on with. I never did quite work out what 'the conditions of late modernity' were, except that they were the conditions in which we lived, about which we had no choice, and that they were largely regrettable (except, perhaps, insofar as they entailed the existence of smartphones with plainchant apps). But it seemed to me (being a bear of very little brain, at least as compared with Father Principal) that the self as an individual, with emotions and preferences and opinions, all belonged to modernity and was therefore a Bad Thing.

So it appeared that I was irredeemably a modern individual, tainted with the suspicion that modern society had actually made not a bad fist of some things on which 2000 years of Christianity had never made much headway (although, of course, a complete hash of some other things), and quite unable to conform myself to the Christian life, even when I was immersed in it up to the eyebrows. I was finding it harder and harder to tell visiting potential students that it was all going to be great. I wasn't even sure I could tell potential Christians it was all going to be great. I echoed the complaint of the Israelites in the wilderness: did God bring me here to let me starve?

— ✳ —

Difficult as that time was, it taught me an important lesson about allowing myself to be vulnerable.

I had been very fortunate to be diagnosed with depression at university, in possibly the most supportive environment possible. The reactions I got after I graduated came as something of a shock—such as the time when my manager, knowing nothing about my own past, expressed his opinion that people with a history of depression shouldn't be in jobs where they make important decisions. (I bit back the retort that it was OK because our job wasn't very important.) My experience at BAP was similar. Eight years after I had taken my last anti-depressant tablet, having never taken time off work for depression in my life, and with no new assessment from anyone medically qualified, I was told that my depression was still too recent and the risks of a similar episode recurring were too high. In retrospect, perhaps I was too honest. I could have blamed my depressive episode on a bad reaction to some other medication, being 19, and a boy with an irresistible penchant for cravats (and who is now a priest in the Ordinariate, the Roman Catholic refuge for ex-Anglican opponents of women's ordination... yeah, I really know how to pick them). All of that would have been true, but instead I admitted that it was statistically quite likely to recur but I would handle it much better. The church opted to stay on the safe side.

The word that's always used in these scenarios is 'robust'. A priest needs to be robust. On the one hand, this is common sense: ordained ministry is demanding and the emotional risks to priest and parishioners alike are high. On the other hand, where does this leave our relationship with the one whose 'power is made perfect in weakness'? There is a lot of talk in the church about valuing vulnerability and weakness, but do we ever dare to live that principle out?

My perception has been that there's a big disparity between physical and mental illness. Those who overcome the limitations of physical illness are characterised as heroic; physical weakness becomes a proof of mental strength. But there seems to be a world of difference, in terms of perception, between the person with arthritis who can't cope with stairs and the person with depression who can't cope with mornings. Sometimes I feel the message the world has for me is the opposite from the one it has for people who face physical challenges: not 'Don't let it beat you! Live your life!' but 'It's OK, don't push yourself. We can manage just fine without you.'

Well, if the church wanted me to be resilient and capable, I could do resilient and capable. I didn't need to bother anybody else with my doubts and fears. I just needed to get on with doing what was in front of me, and on one level I was doing a pretty good job of it: my end-of-year report showed no sign that any inner turmoil had leaked on to the outside. But, as the psalmist says, 'I was mute and silent, I refrained even from good, and my sorrow grew worse' (Psalm 39:2, NASB).

For months, I was impermeable. My pores were closed. I was not able either to receive or to give. It took a long time for me to realise I could let it out gently—just mention in passing that 'I've been overdoing it' or 'I've been stressed about...'. It didn't have to be a big deal. It didn't open a can of worms, of concerned looks and serious conversations and letters to the bishop. On the contrary, it generally turned out that other people were going through all the same things, and as soon as I started talking, I started to feel better. I felt that I was coming out of a very claustrophobic, deadening place, where I couldn't see or feel or do anything properly, into space and light and air. Suddenly, what was tense became malleable; what was congealed became liquid. Christ once stopped up the flow of a woman; for me, he made what had been stopped to flow again. He took away my heart of stone and gave me a heart of flesh. I was capable, for the first time in many months, to feel full compassion, to be moved, to notice and enjoy shapes and colours and details around me, to yearn and to respond lovingly. I remembered that I was in love with my husband. For months I had been unable to grow; in two weeks I grew more than in the whole of the rest of the year. Emotionally and spiritually I was finally back in the building.

The moment of conversion really had been a liberation. My faith made me *happy*. But not being happy all the time didn't mean I was losing my faith. On the contrary, I have come to suspect that dissatisfaction is a human universal. It is because of our fallenness that we are unable to find true joy in the good things that God has given us. Maybe vulnerability is not a regrettable part of ourselves, but a part we need to love, part of the gift we have to offer to others. I still remember the impression made on me by the priest in one gloriously eccentric Welsh parish, who handled the words of the liturgy as gently as if he might bruise them with his lips, and preached about being miserable at Christmas. The transparency of his vulnerability was a transparency to the raw reality of God. Was I really sparing people bother by not letting them minister to me? Or was I jealously keeping myself to myself, when my self was exactly what I was supposed to be pouring out for others—the whole of my self, my needs as well as my strengths?

— ✳ —

There comes a time in any ordinand's training when they just want to run away. So I did.

Most students at my college were there for two years but, because of my age, I got three. That meant most of my year group were already ordained by the time I started my final year. For those of us left behind, what do you do with a third year? Well, much as I loved Mirfield and, for that matter, the Church of England, it seemed to me that we could do with a little time apart—and I guess two years of me was quite enough for the college too, because they suggested I might like to spend a term abroad, in Romania.

Obviously I couldn't just flee the country without some kind of justification, so I came up with a research project that would give an Anglican female ordinand the excuse to be hanging round an Orthodox theological faculty (sans cassock, I was advised). I've come to think, though, that it's valuable simply for an ordinand to spend some time abroad on their own. For one thing, I wanted to know what I would be like, living independently. Well, I learned that within the first week: I'm hopeless. Without a husband and a cat to keep me domesticated, I stayed up past midnight eating unidentifiable foreign delicacies out of jars and drinking 'extra masculine taste' beer (Romanian advertising slogans could do with some work). I reverted to true student behaviour, milk keeping fresh on the windowsill, and movies on my laptop at midnight. But it was something I needed to do—the antidote to the Common Life, the chance to remember how to be an adult with responsibility for my own life.

To paraphrase St John, 'There are many more things which are not written in this book', and this is not the time for a travelog of my Romanian journey. But it was the first time I'd lived in a genuinely Christian country. I could stand in the street by my hostel and see young people making the sign of the cross as they passed the cathedral, quite unself-consciously. It gave me a different perspective on my own church, a totally different set of lenses from the catholic or evangelical ones I was used to looking through. After a week in the monastery of Durau, waking up every morning to a view of mountains and the sound of the *toaca* (wooden bell), eating home-made cheese with *mamaliga* (polenta porridge) and drinking milk warm from the cow, the Christian life looked a lot more appealing, and, frankly, even a life of celibacy didn't seem like such a bad deal. But it also reminded me why I was where I was—that I was a Western Christian, not an Eastern one, and that I had a lot to thank my own Anglican tradition for, not least when it came to the treatment of women.

Two days after I got back from Romania, I was on a plane again—this time to Rome, with a group of fellow students. I had never felt tempted to go before, but now it seemed perfect timing. I wanted to make pilgrimage to the city whose might had been vanquished by the helplessness of the martyrs—the city that conquered the world, only to lay it at the feet of its own crucified victim—and there to seek the blessing of the founding saints of the Church in the West, Peter and Paul, for everything that was to come.

A brace of vocations

As I've said before, one thing I always get asked, as a female ordinand, is whether my husband is ordained. From my Orthodox friends it's an understandable mistake; what other excuse could there be for the beard? From Anglicans, I find it rather peculiar and maybe even slightly offensive. I don't remember anyone asking me, when I told them I worked in Data Protection, if my husband was in information rights too—although, frankly, that might be because they'd already stopped listening.

The implication of the question, it seems to me, is 'Where did you get that idea?' or possibly 'So in your family, is priesthood something normal?' as if being married to someone who had a vocation would at least be a reasonable excuse for having one myself. Being called by God is just too odd an idea, too startling. If I can get a vocation out of the blue, then nobody is safe. Better to assume I caught it through close and prolonged contact.

It does seem to be the case, though, that female clergy are often married to male clergy. Many, of course, met at theological college. Others married in the days when the only way a woman was going to get into the vicarage was to marry the priest. But very often, for whatever reason, the wife only began to explore her own vocation after experiencing the priestly life vicariously (pun fully intended) through her husband. Couples in which the woman was ordained before the man seem to be much rarer.

I was very thankful that we were not going to be a 'clergy couple'. I could always cheerfully answer, 'No: it was all my own idea, and God's.' Laurence's line, when asked the same question, was that he had a strong vocation to be a layman. In fact, I always felt that a lay husband would be something of an asset. Since nobody really knows what the 'vicar's husband' is supposed to do, that would leave him free to be a normal human being and an invaluable link with the world of secular work, which is most people's everyday experience. I had absolutely no desire to be Mr & Mrs Vicar.

God, as usual, had other plans.

A few months before my BAP, a time when one should avoid loud noises and sudden shocks, I suddenly found that there was a second priestly vocation in the Price household. Some people's vocations, like mine, creep up on them; others arrive like a bolt from the blue. I would like to say that I was attentive and supportive when Laurence told me that he too was now exploring this vocation. In fact, I simply filed the idea under 'too big to think about now' and hoped it would clear up by itself. It didn't. Within days, the upstairs cupboard had been re-rigged as a chapel, complete with stations of the cross. He started attending the cathedral daily. Conversations across the kitchen table had become earnest and theological. Fast-forward two years, and here we are planning for yet another total life upheaval. It's getting to be a habit.

On the one hand, it was wonderful that Laurence finally understood what I'd been going through. There were no longer any quibbles about the importance of spending time on church activities, or resentment of my devotional eccentricities. I also realised, now the boot was on the other foot, with what patience he must have borne my inability to talk about anything else. On the other hand, I had absolutely no interest in being a clerical couple. A lay husband was an asset, a novelty, a link with normality. A clerical husband automatically relegated us to the status of buy-one-get-one-free, and it didn't take a genius to work out which of us would be the sidekick.

But, I reasoned, these things take ages to discern. Probably lots of people get false alarms. If God wants it, it'll happen, and if he doesn't, it won't, but right now I don't have time to worry about it. So I flagged it 'worry about later' and got on with the troubles that were sufficient unto the day.

There were plenty of those. Not to put too fine a point on it, theological colleges wreck marriages. Handing out recommendations for marriage guidance counsellors is all in a day's work for the college staff. The unmarried students face their own burdens, of course: the church bureaucracy doesn't yet seem to have got its collective head round the fact that unmarried does not mean under 25 (or, for that matter, necessarily not a parent) and that a professional person in their 30s or 40s might not be able to move everything into a single room, or go 'home' to their parents during the vac. One of the first and most important warnings I was given was that every group in college thinks every other group has it easy.

But at least the ordinands, single or married, have made the choice themselves. The ordinand's spouse may have been peripheral to the discernment process, even peripheral to their partner's spiritual life. After all, there's no requirement that a priest's spouse even be a Christian. Their role until now has been one of supportive bafflement. Then suddenly they find that they're the one being asked to make the biggest changes. They're the one supporting their ordinand spouse financially, taking on the lion's share of child care, and saying goodbye to their home, knowing it will be the last house they ever get a say in choosing.

Even for those couples who aren't physically separated, there is a kind of separation. One of you is entering a new world, a new phase of life, while the other is staying put. The ordinand is having life-changing experiences and intense relationships with their new friends. Their spouse is coming home from work to a conversation full of unfamiliar names, in-jokes and chatter about the *hilarious* thing that happened today with the thurible. My husband was never a jealous person before we came to college, but then I'd never had an emotional fling with 30 other people before.

In a marriage, as in the Common Life, it's in the shared prayer that the underlying dynamics come to the surface. When Laurence and I first started praying together, he was the one who led. He was the one who had been Christian for longer, so it seemed natural that he was the one to say grace, to read the house-blessing at Epiphany, to start off the psalms at Compline. When I was selected for training, without anything being said, I took over, and within weeks, we were living in an institution built round the needs of the ordinands. My husband was 'a spouse' in his own home.

It was an institution, moreover, dedicated to transforming the person he'd married, and not necessarily in ways he had any control over. One of the most significant transitions for me was having to tell Laurence that certain things were pastoral and confidential and I couldn't discuss them with him. Since we had become one flesh in marriage, he'd been used to us being treated as interchangeable; someone would tell something to him or to me, and would assume it meant that the family Price had been informed. The first time I was upset over something I couldn't share, he was angry, but there was nothing I could do. I was trying to minister to others but I could no longer let him minister fully to me.

To the ordinand, all of this tension may be invisible or, at least, go unnoticed. When something is good for us, when we're excited or delighted about something, it's easy to assume it's a good or exciting or delightful thing in itself, when, in fact, for somebody else it might be quite the opposite. For me, coming to college meant new and exciting experiences. For Laurence, it was an hour less in bed and a much more stressful commute. In retrospect, I wasn't sufficiently aware of or alive to that. Everything else in my life was new and changing; it was a relief to have things in my life that represented stability and continuity, and which didn't (I thought) need constant input from me to keep them going. In my mind, my husband became one of those settled things, one of the things that was already sorted out, in the bag, like my degree or my driving licence. My relationship with my husband was the most important thing in my life, but right now I was busy. My marriage would just have to stay put until I got back to it.

Except that my husband—his faith, his life, his plans—was actually changing rather rapidly. Once I got round to noticing that it was really happening, I belatedly remembered to be extremely excited about my husband's vocation. From the outside, and from the comfortable position of having it all safely behind me, it all seemed a lot more like a thrilling adventure than I remembered, and a lot less like siege warfare. Like looking through a childhood photo album, I could relive all the fun bits, safe in the knowledge that I would never, ever have to go through that again.

It was also rather disconcerting. It was all going on without me. For the last couple of years, I'd been the centre of attention in our household as far as ministry and vocation were concerned. It was quite a lesson in humility to see it all from the outside and experience for myself what I must have put Laurence through two years previously. My expectations for my life were about to be turned upside down (again) and it was all being calmly decided in a series of meetings in Manchester, without any need for my input. 'Calmly' is the word: in comparison with me, Laurence seemed to sail through it quite unperturbed, or at least with a lot less need to talk about it incessantly.

Stranger still was seeing Laurence himself in a different light. 'Darling, I've got a vocation' is a little bit like 'Darling, I'm pregnant.' There is something inside the person you love which is probably wonderful but is certainly going to change both your lives, and the person you thought you knew better than anyone is going to become something—a mother, a priest—that they weren't before. I first knew it was serious when Laurence's daily office, for the first time, actually became *daily*, something that two or three years of my good example hadn't managed to encourage in him. When it came to considering where he might want to study, he casually mentioned the idea that he might want to do a doctorate one day. This was the same guy who had always prided himself on being a generalist—meaning someone with more important things to do than essays. He got his best essay mark on one course (to my certain knowledge) by pulling an all-nighter in the library after his tutor phoned *me* up to say he'd missed the deadline. This was the new serious

Laurence. Other people were taking this Laurence seriously, and I needed to as well.

So, three years after I'd been there myself, I waved off my husband (equipped with the essential earplugs) to the same retreat centre, the same ordeals and, as it turned out, even the same pastoral exercise I had faced. I'm a natural back-seat driver, but there he was beyond my advice, influence or anything but the occasional anxious phone call or good-luck text—and all I achieved with that was to make his phone go off just as he was starting his presentation. All of this was probably no bad thing, since (as I've several times had to inform startled BAP candidates seeking my advice) I am about the single worst person to advise on the BAP. If he got through, he would have succeeded where I never had and never will.

The news came through on a frosty mid-November evening. It was a 'Yes'. For certain good reasons, Laurence was not able to tell me straight away. So it happened that the first I heard of Laurence's good news was also my first experience of being 'the spouse' in the relationship. I was used to being the one who had to keep confidences. Now our roles had been reversed: he was the one with a new life that I was not part of, and secrets that I could not be party to. I was unprepared for how much of a knock that would be. I didn't even succeed in commandeering the celebrations with a grand announce-ment and champagne. He was so coy and modest that, even when somebody asked him directly, I had to jump up and down behind him, pointing and grinning and giving thumbs-up, just so they got the message.

My first reaction, of course, was great joy for him. My second was to feel curiously erased, as if someone had followed in my footsteps wearing bigger shoes. 'My' vocational journey was obliterated and replaced by 'ours'. Something that, for me, had been a struggle, he had apparently breezed through. My vocational journey had felt like a daring and difficult process, something nobody I knew had ever done, a precious and terrifying secret that blossomed into an almost unbelievable adventure. Now, seeing it from the outside, it looked like a perfectly normal and obvious thing to do. In fact, if you are living in a theological college, it really is what everybody does. I found myself wondering what I'd been making such a fuss about.

The excitement of Laurence's news eclipsed anything that was going on in my life. Laurence heard from the diocese that he'd been accepted on the very day I agreed with the same diocese that I wouldn't be coming back (of which more later). For a diocese to gain one ordinand and lose another from the same family on the same day may be some kind of record—but that was no longer the latest news, even for me. I was relegated to page 2 in my own life.

It says something about the way college has changed our relationship that, three years ago, we categorically said we wouldn't live apart while I was at college. Now, Laurence is preparing to go to college and I'm preparing to spend at least half of each week without him. It's a sign of the strength we have in being able to trust one another—and remember that marriage (like joy) is measured in years, not just in days—but it's also, perhaps, a sign of something that's been lost along the way, or maybe given up.

I am told that the reason the Orthodox place crowns on the heads of newlyweds is to symbolise the crown of martyrdom. Compared with a life of celibacy, let alone facing the lions in the Coliseum, marriage might seem like the easy option, the second-class route to holiness. But for those who are called to it, it is equally the context for the sacrificial life. Marriage is a form of community living, the Common Life at its most intense and inescapable. It entails compromise, which is, in a little way, the death of the self for the sake of the other. But it also means the death of false others, the illusory husbands and wives of our imagination. Of all the things I have found most difficult to give to God, by far the hardest has been my husband. I wouldn't give up my ordinand husband for the world, not even for the mountains of Romania, but perhaps celibacy and cheese-making might have been simpler!

Deal or no deal

One morning, the Principal addressed a few words of advice to those of us who were shortly to enter our final year. He began like a kindly patriarch warning his virgin daughters about the snares of the world. We had probably already begun to receive phone calls from dioceses seeking to poach us from our sponsoring bishops (this was news to me), but, he admonished us, we must remember that we were not free to arrange our curacies by ourselves. We must resist all flattery and temptation and rely in all things on the wise guidance of the college.

I was astounded. I had no idea that curates were such a sought-after commodity. I was also a little bit scared. Might this naïve ordinand unwittingly fall prey to the shady world of black-market curacies? Like a virtuous daughter, I braced myself to repulse the attentions of unwanted suitors—and was slightly put out that nobody had yet given me the opportunity.

The chances of my being swept off my feet by a tall dark bishop were fairly small. Even in the C of E, where everyone knows everyone, I had achieved almost complete obscurity. How would a diocesan headhunter even know of my existence? Nevertheless, it was a reminder to start looking to the future. I had almost forgotten it, but the whole point of going to college was to leave it again.

— ✳ —

Once upon a time, the curate was an extra pairs of hands in the parish, employed at the whim of the incumbent. What little I knew of the role was gleaned from historical novels and seemed to consist mostly of providing the plot with a respectable but impecunious bachelor, the male social equivalent of the governess. He hung around playing second-fiddle to a more senior or more well-connected clergyman, until such time as he could find a living of his own and afford to make an offer to the heroine. Curates belonged in Barchester, not in Salford or Stepping Hill—until, that is, I found myself in line to become one.

Curacy nowadays, of course, is a little bit different. It exists for the sake of the trainee's future ministry, not the convenience of a parish priest—and of course, there is a Process. As with selection and formation, your curate comes to you thoroughly processed, the human equivalent of Dairylea.

The system for matching curates and training places is modelled on the popular game show, *Deal or No Deal?* The banker—or, in this case, the bishop—has a box containing parishes, but the candidate is not allowed to see what is inside. Instead, they are made an offer, which they must then accept or refuse. If they accept, they may unknowingly have turned down the chance of their ideal parish. If they refuse, they might get a better offer—but they also run the risk of being told there's nothing for them. It's edge-of-the-sofa stuff.

At least, as a three-year student, I had some chance of actually being formed by my formation before I was matched up with my future curacy, but this next stage felt very different from what had gone before. The paperwork for BAP had been exhaustive and exhausting. Everything had been about discernment—thorough, spiritual and very slow indeed. Now the challenge was the opposite: to summarise myself, my training needs and my hopes for my future ministry in three tickboxes. The main thing the form revealed about me was how well (or not) the past few years had taught me to speak C of E code. What is the difference between traditional catholic and modern catholic? Is it (a) drum kit, (b) women, or (c) *Common Worship*? And which one, traditional or modern, am I? I decided to tick both.

That was my total input into the selection of my first potential curacy match—the equivalent of the three questions in *Blind Date*. I felt something like a bride anticipating an arranged marriage. Was I about to be introduced to my perfect match or was I going to end up on the shelf?

There are many ways in which an ordination is like a marriage. You can't go to your parish priest and say you want to get married just because you want to be a married person. You have to have someone to get married to. Just as you can't get married in general, but only to a specific person, so you can't be ordained except to a specific community. That goes right back to the Council of Chalcedon in AD451, in case you were wondering. No curacy, no ordination.

I might not actually be in a Trollope novel, but the idea of finding a curacy put me in romantic spirits nonetheless. I imagined first hearing the name of my future church over the phone, then tearing open the post to read the glossy parish profile. A tentative first date; love at first sight; the formal proposal on diocesan headed notepaper... Somewhere out there was my future curacy. Somewhere out there, a priest and a parish were praying for someone they didn't yet know was me. I was looking forward to a long courtship.

But I wasn't going to be fussy. A standard topic of conversation for a couple of weeks concerned red lines. How far would you be prepared to move? Are you bothered about what the house is like? Would you refuse to settle for anything less than Mass every day and Benediction on Sundays? My only baggage was a cat, a husband and minimal standards of liturgical taste and decency. For once, I wasn't going to be the awkward one.

Right?

So I had a name—the name of my potential curacy.

I tried to be enthusiastic. After the struggle of selection, the intensity of college, the travels I was still looking forward to, perhaps anything would seem underwhelming. Perhaps I needed to be more realistic. After all, I would be there to feed the flock, not to seek spiritual nourishment for myself. Maybe, like a caterpillar about to transform into a butterfly, I was due to shed my mouthparts, to live on the store of spiritual energy I'd already built up. I'd had my years of living the crazy dream; maybe now I needed to settle down, rediscover my professionalism and get back to doing a stable job.

If only that didn't feel so different from what God had been trying to teach me for the past few years.

The parish did sound like a nice place, with a highly competent incumbent. It just didn't sound like anywhere I had imagined myself going. I was flummoxed. What part of 'as urban as you like, as catholic as you dare' had they not understood? A phone call to the diocese followed, and the voice at the other end of the line took on that slightly weary, bewildered tone common to those who have had to deal with my selection and formation. The voice sounded as baffled by my question as I was by the answer. Apparently, this church was 'eucharistic'. As in what? It celebrates the Eucharist? So, it's a church. What would it be if it *weren't* eucharistic? And there was to be no parish profile and no courtship; even attending a service was considered an optional precaution. I felt like I'd come down to earth with a bump.

I was advised to make a decision about the parish 'on its own merits'. When you move house at the diocese's expense, they expect three quotes from removals companies. If you are merely choosing a curacy, you get one option, take it or leave it.

I wanted to make the humble and obedient decision, whatever that was. Failing that, *any* decision—anything that would put an end to the uncertainty. But I was afraid that any decision I made would be based on fear of the unknown. I just wished someone else would make the decision for me—preferably God, of course, but the DDO or Laurence or frankly anybody else would do.

On the face of it, the question seemed a simple one: is God calling me to this place? That was the only question that mattered. God, of course, had not deserted me, but my instinct had. It was as if I'd gone into a jeweller's shop to get a watch and the salesman had offered me a bracelet instead. It was a perfectly nice bracelet. So here I was, seriously considering a bracelet 'on its own merits', when what I really needed was a watch.

By the time I had my formal meeting with the incumbent, I had already decided it probably wouldn't work. So had she. It was the first of many things we agreed on. In fact, we agreed on so many things, we ended up thinking maybe it could work after all. But I wasn't going into ordained ministry because I wanted a different job, a congenial way to support myself. I had to go where I was really needed. I felt guilty for refusing to do the sensible, respectable thing, like Lizzie Bennet turning down Mr Collins. However, as Laurence put it, I was only stringing the diocese along. Just because a guy's a nice guy, or a parish is a nice parish, and you think you *ought* to like it, if there's no chemistry it's going nowhere.

So I had to say goodbye to the diocese that had supported me through so much. The DDO called me while I was standing in the car park of a mosque, on a college interfaith study trip. When I said that my hijab was making it hard to hear, he responded, 'Well, I knew you were thinking of leaving the diocese...'! More seriously, he also reminded me that I now had no diocese and no guarantee I'd even get ordained this year. I was on my own.

Humility sounds like a great idea when you hear it ascribed to the saints. After all, they were humble and now they're famous, right? We forget that most humble people, by definition, have been forgotten—and most probably went unnoticed in the first place. One of the most humbling things about entering the clergy, and therefore one of the hardest, is that your achievements don't count for anything. Curacies are not competitive; you do not need to have higher marks or a longer CV than the next person, and it wouldn't help if you did. But that can lead to a feeling that you are not valued as an individual. Dioceses aren't interested in getting the best curates for the best curacies, since there's officially no such thing. They just need to fit us all in somewhere. I wasn't an asset, just a slightly annoying logistical problem.

By the time I got back from my summer placement, most of my friends were already sorted for curacies. Not all were happy, but all were glad the decision was made. It took me a while to realise that what I was feeling was envy—and it took a conversation with my spiritual director to find out that the feeling is completely standard. Meanwhile, I was waiting to see where Laurence might end up, and, since he had not yet come clean about his forthcoming BAP, I could only say enigmatically that there were good reasons why my curacy was delayed. People nodded and looked sympathetic, and wondered what was wrong with me.

Then I got a message from the Principal. The DDO of a certain diocese had been reading my blog. But curacy nego- tiations are top secret, so, for a couple of mad weeks, my life became a low-budget thriller—all urgent phone calls and whispers in corridors, sudden train journeys and off-the- record conversations. The East Coast via Doncaster had never been so thrilling! I went into the interview as if I had nothing to lose. Half an hour of heated debate later, amazingly, the rector still wanted to offer me the post.

I had been hoping to indulge in a long process of discernment. I'd even looked up Ignatius Loyola's technique, as recommended for decisions just such as this, and it looked set to satisfy my obsession for several weeks. In the end, though, the decision had to be made very quickly. There was no time to pray for guidance, only to pray that God would accept my decision, made with the advice of wise people around me, and would bless it.

Suddenly it was all *very* official. There were more phone calls, more trains, an interview with the bishop. Then there I was, the curate-designate of a town on the east coast, miles from where I'd lived before, miles from where Laurence was going to be, miles from anywhere. Was this the church of God's dreams for me? Was I the curate he had been preparing just for them? I didn't know and I still don't. What I knew was that my heart lifted when I saw it, standing proud against the sea and the centuries, between the wide flat land and the wide flat sea. I didn't know if God was calling me there, but I did know I wanted to pray in it, and for it, and maybe write bad poetry about it. And maybe that is love.

We had a deal.

God and the bishop willing

I started writing this book not knowing if I would finish it. That's not just because of my tendency to procrastinate—although I knew I was in trouble round about the middle of the previous chapter when I started buying oven cleaner—but because I couldn't know for sure that I would be getting ordained.

The phrase we use is, 'God and the bishop willing.' 'When are you getting ordained?' 'June, God and the bishop willing'; 'I'll get a dog after I'm ordained, God and the bishop willing…'. Ordinands are not, as a general rule, superstitious (our heads are full of enough difficult truths to leave little space for easy nonsense), but I found myself using the words compulsively, as if to avert misfortune. I have known two people whose ordinations were cancelled late in the day, so late that the commemorative edition of the *Church Times* had already gone to press. Reading their names there felt like receiving a letter addressed to someone who'd died. So accepting money to write a book leading up to and including my ordination seemed absurdly presumptuous. I wanted to add a clause into the contract: 'God and the bishop willing.'

In Mirfield, naturally, we observe all the proprieties.

Several weeks before Petertide, I was already seeing Facebook events for other people's ordinations and being asked about my own. But I was waiting—waiting for a discreet, one-line note to appear on the Principal's noticeboard: 'You may now distribute your Ember cards.'

According to ordination etiquette, an ordination is not announced with anything so vulgar as an invitation or a notice in the newspaper. It is announced in a modest, circumlocutory and very British way, by means of a small card requesting the prayers of your friends and acquaintances—which just so happens to mention the time and place of your ordination, your new address, and the prospect of light refreshments. So that small, understated note on the board means that the Principal will be recommending us to our respective bishops for ordination. It means we have got through, and neither God nor the bishop has thought better of it. It is a modest, circumlocutory, very British way of saying 'YOU MADE IT!!'

So we come full circle. Three years after I first donned a cassock, I once again have the clerical outfitters' catalogues in my pigeonhole. This time, though, I'm looking at clerical shirts with dog collars. The blouses all have names like Audrey, Beryl or Marjorie. They are ladies-of-the-parish names, friendly but a little bit frumpy. The message is clear: getting ordained is an immediate free pass to middle age.

I'd seen it happen to two sets of friends already. You say goodbye to them one bleary morning at the end of term, deeply hung over and trying to pretend that stain on their cassock isn't what it smells like. The next time you see them, they are wearing a crisp white surplice and the only spirit that's anointing them is the Spirit of God. One month they are a student, the next, a bona fide Minister of Religion, with a dog collar and a special tax code and a reduced car insurance premium, the kind of person who can give you a character reference and sign the back of your passport photo. Now it was my turn. After three years in captivity, I was due to be released into the wild as a Deacon.

The Deacon—otherwise known as somebody who spends a year explaining that no, actually they're not the vicar. This story started with my calling to the priesthood, but it ends (as far as you are concerned, dear reader) with my ordination to the diaconate.

I remember the very first ordination I went to, some years before I became a Christian, feeling rather short-changed that my husband's friend was not a priest at the end of it but some other thing called a deacon. I also made the mistake of starting in on the buffet without waiting for the grace. The diaconate has an honourable place in the Bible: it was the deacons, not the bishops, who contributed the first martyr. But some time between then and the Book of Common Prayer, it got the reputation of an 'inferior office', a mere precursor to priestly ordination. As a deacon, I'll be able to bless objects but not people (there was some debate over whether I could bless the cat). I'll take baptisms but not weddings. I will be able to wear my stole on one shoulder but not on two, held together diagonally (or, rather, diaconally) with a little loop or hook. It looks unhelpfully, and inaccurately, like being only half-ordained—as if we've simply got an extra year of maturing to do before we develop into full priests. As they would say in the Grolsch advert: 'Shtop! This priest is not ready yet!'

That gave me just a few weeks to break the habit of the past five years, of talking about priesthood and ordination as if they were the same thing. Having responded to a call to the priesthood, convinced at least some people that I was meant to be a priest, and been formed for the priesthood, I was about to become something else, something for which I didn't feel prepared at all. It was yet another of those unwelcome humblings.

This being the Church of England, of course, this life-changing sacramental transformation must be followed by refreshments.

Technically, I'm sure that the ordination would still be valid even if no more than a cup of tea were provided, but that would not do justice to the gravity of the occasion. Being permanently set apart for the service of God calls, at the very least, for a buffet. Assorted cold pork products are the traditional British way of marking important life events—although ordinands from the diocese of Europe have no such reservations. After last year's ordination season, I was left with a firm desire never to eat another sausage roll in my life—and with a pair of pink flashing bunny ears...

Laurence, in spite of being a lifelong Anglican, has never quite got on with the catering aspect of English religion. The sight of a custard cream and an inoffensive cup of Fairtrade instant after divine service is enough to make him suddenly recall an appointment elsewhere or an urgent spiritual need for silence and contemplation. He was all in favour of ditching the reception and having a quiet night in. Perhaps he was afraid that I would go crazy and spend my pre-ordination retreat making panicked phone calls about table centrepieces. I saw it differently. It would be my first act as a deacon: extending hospitality to those who had accompanied me on my journey to this point and those whom I would be serving with in the future. It would be a reminder that my big day was not all about me at all.

I'm not good at last times. I'm not talking about *the* Last Times, the *parousia*. I mean, the way that doing something you've done scores of times before takes on a new and special poignancy when you realise that it might never happen again. I found myself tearing up at the most banal things: you mean I'm *never* going to wash up after Thursday night dinner *ever again*?! This bus ticket was my *last ever* day saver on the 203?!

Then there are the slightly more significant 'lasts'—like my last Christmas.

I'd expected Christmas to be bigger and more special since I'd finally followed the advice of countless church posters and put Christ back into it, but, actually, the joy that my faith gives to the season is of a rather solemn sort. It doesn't seem quite appropriate any more to indulge in all the peripheral excesses, once so central to my festive celebrations, such as the annual fruit and nut selection binge, usually the one time in the year when I decide I like salted pistachios. In fact, Christians like to mark their faith commitment by pouring the cold water of Advent on what would otherwise be the festive season. Even so, my final Christmas before ordination felt like a 'last'. Most clergy spend Advent serving up Christmas-on-demand three times weekly, with no time to prepare for their own because they're too busy writing that sermon about not getting too busy at Christmas. The good old secular English Christmas spirit, part of my life for 30 years, has visited my household for the final time.

I'm also saying goodbye to colour. Perhaps it's fortunate that I spent nearly three months living out of a suitcase and have forgotten how to pick what to wear in the mornings. As of June, my wardrobe will be like Henry Ford's production line: any colour I like, so long as it's black. Of course, not every curate wears black all the time. In fact, my incumbent's only sartorial advice was not to wear episcopal purple. But in Romania, I learned, the sign of a priest (or, indeed, a nun) is not a little square of white plastic but the colour black, symbolic of death. So I felt that dying to colour was a sacrifice I ought to make.

Nothing has brought it home to me that my life is about to change quite as much as looking at dresses in the shops and realising there's no point buying any of them. My love of colour will need to be rechannelled into my clerical curtain collection, which, according to one of my tutors, every clergyperson has—a pile of curtains that fitted one of your previous vicarages and might possibly fit one of the future ones. And I don't rule out the occasional colourful scarf or jacket, so maybe I'm not quite dead to the world, just very poorly. I'm also about to commit to spending the rest of my life wearing a high collar with a big bust. Trinny and Susannah, I am so sorry.

But ordination means firsts as well as lasts. When I tried on a clerical shirt for the first time (described as 'modern fit', so I was only slightly swamped), I automatically thought, 'I look like a priest!' And then remembered: 'Oops, no, a deacon!'

In the last week of the year, there is a special service to bless the ordination stoles. Lined up over the bench are ten or twelve strips of cloth, each one representing an ordinand. The fun bit is trying to guess whose is whose. The designs of the stoles represent something of what we've come to value during our formation and what will shape us in our ministry to come. I have seen stoles that celebrate the wearer's entire spiritual journey in appliqué, though at Mirfield it tends to be a bit more subtle and therefore more of a challenge. Still, I sometimes think you learn more about a person's spirituality and the way they see their ministry from their stole and their Ember card than from living with them for two years. Mine arrived too late to join the line-up for the fashion parade, but what it most expressed was my failure to imbibe the spirit of ascetical simplicity. It was almost as delicious to describe as to look at: deep cream Florence brocade with Holbein orphreys in Canterbury Blue and cream tassels, the haberdashery equivalent of a brownie sundae with cream *and* sprinkles.

It's as if, having been trained in conformity and the common life, our individuality is suddenly reblossoming. Having travelled this journey together, we will arrive at our common destination in different places, on different days, and with different companions. On this most important day, we are not able to be there to support one another. We will be part of a new community—our new fellow deacons in each diocese.

Our time at college ended not with evensong, but with Mattins and Mass. With the light of a new day shining through the windows of the chapel, we shared our final Communion. And, as we had done so many times before, we heard the words of the sending out: 'Go in the peace of Christ'. Only this time, we went.

Revving up

Three years ago, before I set off for college, a colleague wished me luck for my 'collaring'. It took me a moment to realise she meant ordination. It's appropriate: a pigeon is ringed round its foot, a bull through the nose and a bride on her finger, and we clergy are ringed round the neck. Those who study the theology of ordination talk of it as an 'indelible mark' on the soul. What it meant was that the course I had chosen was about to become irreversible.

Jesus' ministry did not start immediately after his baptism. Having received that affirmation from God, he then had to pay a call on the other guy, to receive the back-handed compliment of renewed opposition and testing. Ordinands receive the affirmation of their vocation in the form of a report rather than a dove and a voice from heaven, but for us too there is a gap before our active ministry starts, and for us too it is a renewed time of testing.

It's not quite a wilderness but there is a curious emptiness, an absence of familiar landmarks. In those few days between the end of term and moving house, I woke up still in Mirfield but no longer at Mirfield. My house was full of cards addressed to someone who did not yet exist: 'The Reverend K. Price'. Everyday decisions made me stumble. Do I wear my cassock? Do I still have to attend public worship on a Sunday evening? Am I lying if I fill in this form as a student?

There was no difference between this week and the same week in summer the previous year, and yet there was every difference, because I would not be coming back next term. I missed Mirfield already, in that special way that one can miss a place in anticipation, and I took the time to miss it, knowing that once I left I would be on to a new chapter and wouldn't look back.

The statutory period of temptation began. Over the course of a month I was confronted, one way or another, with pretty much everything that scared me about what was to come and everything that made me look over my shoulder at other lives I could have had. It was like a personalised tour of every challenge or doubt or regret that had ever made me question the path I was taking. Often, my friends and well-wishers were the unwitting means by which temptation made its entrance. The deacons with tales of their first year in curacy. The old university friend whose beautifully furnished new house represented an ideal of adulthood I would never attain. The kindly parishioner who paid a call on the frazzled new curate while the removal van was still in the driveway and brought home to me that our lives were now public property.

And that was how I found myself, on D-minus-16, sitting on the sofa with tea and home-made cake, utterly terrified.

I wanted to feel thankful for this huge house, for the windows that left a gap at the bottom of my curtains, the lightbulbs dangling out of my reach as I stood on a chair, and the wide choice of rooms in which to forget that I'd left my handbag or my keys. Instead, it was just a reminder of how absurdly oversized this life was. Everything about being a curate was wonderful but (like some of my new clerical clothes) cut for a bigger person than me.

— ✳ —

By the time I set out for my pre-ordination retreat, I was ready to call the whole thing off. Most of us had suffered doubts along the way; I'd saved them all up for maximum impact.

The night before my retreat, we had sausages. I'm told it's a favourite last supper for condemned criminals. The intended significance was the opposite: it was the first meal in a fortnight that didn't involve a microwave or a takeaway menu, and it was supposed to mark a new start. New home, new role, new cooker—and what better way to celebrate moving to Lincolnshire than with sausages? But what I was about to do seemed so final, so irrevocable, more like an execution than the start of a new life. When a friend sent me a text saying 'See you on the other side!' it seemed hilariously, morbidly appropriate. I set off from my new house as if I were setting off on my final journey, unable to shake the feeling that I would never see it again with the same eyes.

I was looking forward to being back in community again, a community praying together, all in the same boat. Then one of my fellow ordinands commented on how odd it must be for me, 'coming into it so late on', and I felt the sudden shock of my perceptions crashing against his. Most of these people had trained together, right here, on the local course. For them, this was another chapter in a long companionship. We college students were incomers, blundering in on their last week of term. They were 'us'; we were 'them'. Never had I missed the Common Life so much.

But there is one place that remains home for an ex-Mirfield student, and it can be found anywhere. After supper on the first evening, we entered silence. I slipped into it gratefully, as comfortable and familiar as my old cassock. I knew absolutely nothing about being a deacon; put on the spot, I could not bring to mind a single thing I'd been taught that was going to help me do my job, come Monday morning. Yet here was one thing at which I'd had plenty of practice.

In the silence, face to face with God for what felt like the first time in a long while, I took stock. In every area of my life I saw change. There was nothing left to provide stability, nothing that equipped me or nourished me, nothing to be the anchor on these new seas. The geography of my life was as unfamiliar as the flat lands of Lincolnshire after the West Yorkshire hills. And now my husband, the one person I might reasonably expect to be my rock, I felt was being taken away. He might have the same old face I knew and loved, but those eyes were looking towards a new future in September, in a new town and with new friends. Even my name was unfamiliar. I had agreed with my incumbent that I would be 'Katherine' in the parish, having been Katy since birth, and there is nothing to make you look and feel more stupid than having to correct yourself every time you introduce yourself by the wrong name. It was as if I had set out on a journey and had neglected to bring anything with me, even my name.

Since I have a talent for grandiose self-pity, as well as access to rather a nice walled garden, I decided to meditate on the agony at Gethsemane. But the passage that leaped out at me was one I had never taken notice of before, one that had always been hidden by the hugeness of the other events around it.

He said to them, 'When I sent you out without a purse, bag, or sandals, did you lack anything?' 'Nothing,' they answered (Luke 22:35).

— ✳ —

Jesus, before he was crucified, was first stripped. Perhaps a kind of stripping is also involved in our call to take up the cross. I am wary of drawing such a parallel; in the abstract, our aspiration to share in the sufferings of Christ can be yet another temptation to aggrandise ourselves and our own lives, but the reality, as ever, is mundane and unasked-for. Most of us, thank God, are not called to lives of heroic suffering; God knows of what we are made. But there is a little low way of the cross, a path built for small and well-heeled feet, and paved with the sharp stones of everyday disappointments. I always said I wanted to come to Christ as an empty vessel, with literally nothing, but I hadn't realised this was what I was asking for—to come with nothing to offer whatsoever, knowing myself not just unworthy of the task laid before me but completely incompetent for it.

The sacrifice of God is a broken spirit. We all go into ordination expecting sacrifice; what we are not told is the nature of the sacrifice that will be asked of us. The real sacrifice for me was not, in the end, anything to do with money or status, freedom or security. It was the small things. The compensations I looked forward to in ministry. The little indulgences I thought I needed to sustain myself. All the sources of pride and pleasure, the ulterior motives, the fringe benefits. Everything, that is, that I might desire or rely on apart from God.

We all want to do God's will, but to want it *only* because it's God's will—there's the rub. I never wanted to get ordained, but, once I'd agreed to it, I found there were things I did want. A new cassock. An ordination party. A double gin... Even the desire to do God's will can be an ulterior motive, if it is done for the sake of the peace and certainty that might come with it.

I would like to be able to offer to God my success—an offering in which I would be glorified almost as much as him. Instead, I can offer him only my constant struggles, my fallings-short, an offering that is costly but hardly impressive. We are a broken church in a broken world, stumbling along, seeing through a glass darkly, and all I have to offer to God is my failure.

I woke to the sound of bells—seven great rings breaking like ripples over my bed, as Lincoln Cathedral gave me my own personal wake-up call. For a moment I was back in Romania, where they pipe the chanting of monks into the street, the churches exhaling praises, like spiritual lungs. Now, once more, I woke up to air coloured with God.

There was another sound too, in my mind's ear at least. Each day of my retreat, I woke up with an earworm. On the second day, it was 'How great thou art!' The first day, it had been 'Nowhere to run'!

One of the challenges for me, throughout my discernment, has been the Church of England's apparent embarrassment at the seriousness of what it's about. Sometimes it's just downright naff, but every now and again it unexpectedly rises to the occasion, and one of those occasions is ordination. There is no covering up 'how great is the charge', in the words of the ordinal, which we must be ready to take on.

The day before the service, we donned our cassocks and filed into the chapel to make our solemn oaths to the Queen, the Bishop and the Church. The gravitas was only slightly punctured when I spotted the little logo on the Bible:

apparently, even in a diocesan hotel, we have to rely on the good offices of the Gideons. There the bishop solemnly charged us not to get drunk in public and not to wear jeans and jumpers to important meetings. It was precisely because they were such trivial things that it all felt so weighty; once, these things didn't matter, but now they do. Perhaps my private-sector friends face similar codes of conduct, but it was still a reminder that we were entering something bigger than ourselves, in which other people's expectations and preconceptions would weigh more heavily.

Putting that collar round my neck was the hardest moment for me of the whole event. I stared at the inoffensive strip of white plastic until I was about to be late. Once round my neck, it had a remarkable and immediate effect on my whole being. I walked taller; I sat up straighter. But it wasn't that I was mindful of a new responsibility or dignity—just that every time I slumped, it choked me. The bishop had told us to mind our posture; I hadn't realised the alternative was asphyxiation. Only when I saw how natural everybody else looked did I realise I must look that way to others.

For the rehearsal, we had entered the cathedral through a side door. Now that the real thing was upon us, we lined up outside the great West front. Surplices flapped in the wind. A few passers-by halted in curious clusters, camera-phones in hand. As I looked into that huge space, the stone ribs vaulting the centuries, I felt a kind of vertigo. The space that had been quite navigable at the rehearsal seemed to have been magnified by CGI, as for a Harry Potter film or a Disney princess wedding—except that this was really happening. We stepped into it like parachutists stepping off a plane. There would be no way back.

There was nothing in the service to give credence to the

sense of being half-ordained. When the ordinal says that we share in Christ's ministry, it doesn't just mean a ministry *like* Christ's. It means that ministry which began on the banks of the Jordan and in Galilee: good news for the poor, sight to the blind, freedom to the oppressed. A deacon is called to embody the servanthood of Christ. Nothing of that could be a mere final-year training project. There was a sense of standing between the world and the church, reaching out to each, constantly calling the church back to its responsibility for the vulnerable. I won't stop looking forward to the day I can snip that little hook off the side of my stole—if God and the bishop are still up for it. But the bishop prayed for us as those set apart for the service of God; this was the day that changed my life—my name, my wardrobe, me.

Out of the whole service, strangely, the most profound moment was something I had experienced dozens of times before. At Communion, it was the role of the new deacons to minister the chalice. Over the last few years, I've done this regularly, and it is always a joy and a privilege, but this time I felt a special connection with each person who came to receive. It was a joy and privilege not just to minister, but to minister *to them*—the proper joy and privilege of the deacon.

Ordained ministry is not what I expected. I'm not even sure I can say it's what I wanted—which is probably exactly as it should be.

People ask me if I feel like a different person. The answer is yes—but, again, not in the way I expected. I don't feel like some newly empowered spiritual superhero. I feel like I've just regenerated, Doctor Who style, and have to get my tongue round a new set of teeth. Things I'd done a million times before became, for a fortnight or so, cripplingly difficult. Every time I opened my mouth, I had a brief terror that I might not be able to remember how to speak. I couldn't speak because I didn't know who I was—who I was to these people, in this context. It was as if I'd lost my voice, as if I was trying to speak with somebody else's tongue.

Things that I thought would be easy are hard, and sometimes things I thought would be hard are easy. That dratted collar, for instance. I have always liked clergy to wear their collars, rather than sneaking round in mufti to the discomfiture of unsuspecting atheists. I was expecting it to give me confidence in striking up conversations, the way a name-badge does at a networking event. Instead, I spent a fortnight feeling horribly self-conscious in what suddenly felt uncomfortably like a symbol of authority. Being 'the Reverend', on the other hand, quite unexpectedly felt instantly natural. It was something that had worried me in advance—having no obvious form of address, as a woman, in a parish where the men are 'Father'. The one title I thought I knew I didn't want is the one I legally had to have: 'Rev'. The idea of anybody revering me just seemed laughable. Yet that has turned out to be a non-issue. I've found I don't care what people call me, and I now happily answer to Christine, Caroline and vicar-lady—although my favourite has to be the double-take from somebody who'd just called me Father.

Nothing really prepares you for this—for how difficult it is, but also how straightforward. You spend two or three years learning the theory and looking at the way things are done by various churches and clergy. You reflect on it, you discuss it, you think about how you would do it... and then, when your turn comes, you just do it. Not in the way you were taught or the way you'd decided was best, just whatever way they do it here. On my very first day in post, I got up with a household full of guests, and any questions about what the new and allegedly reverend me would wear or how she would act or whether she would make a good first impression were eclipsed by the questions of how she was going to fix the shower and get into work on time. We say morning prayer with a businesslike momentum, gobbling it down like toast on the way to the bus stop. Baptisms and funerals are routine operations. I didn't learn to take a funeral from a lecture but from my colleague in the car on the way back from meeting a bereaved family. I go into the office and hot-desk and make tea and fight the quirks of the email system, just as I did in the public sector world I left behind.

One recurrent theme that alarms me is how frequently clerical colleagues, on hearing where I studied, josh me that they'll 'soon get me out of all that'. It isn't the most encouraging thing, in your first week in a new job, to be repeatedly told that everything you've learned in the past three years will need to be unlearned. The things that have become precious to us as ordinands are the things we are expected to get over, now that we are ordained. That's a very odd feeling—to come out qualified and formed (supposedly), only to find ourselves a source of amusement to those who have seen many a generation of rookie clergy before.

I suspect I am making myself a hostage to fortune by publishing this book at all. By the time it's on the shelves or in the online shopping trolley, I may well have very different views; there's no point going into three years of curacy not wanting to be changed. Yet I do not want to grow out of what has been entrusted to me at Mirfield; I want to grow into it. At the moment, perhaps that tradition is an oversized garment on me, somewhat absurd and costume-ish. The answer, though, is not to drop it but to live up to it. Am I here to have the rough edges knocked off me? I'm not so sure I want to be palatable and easy to swallow. If I need straightening out on the anvil of parish ministry, let me at least be sharpened like the 'double-edged sword'.

The first sermon I ever preached was on the passage 'My yoke is easy and my burden is light' (Matthew 11:30). The first sermon I preached as a curate was on the same passage, but they were very different sermons.

I wanted an easy life. What God has given me is life itself, life in abundance. Sometimes, it feels like too much life to handle! I've spent my first summer as a curate trying to keep my head above water, the bank balance in the black, the car on the road, and the lawn in check. (Since we're talking of life abundant, the unstoppable growth of my garden has drawn worried comments from parishioners and provided me with the theme of my harvest sermon.) I'm still drinking tea and eating cake and I'm still pretty much completely terrified. I am still not quite sure what God has brought me here for or whether I've been worth the effort. All I know is that any God who could put up with me this far is in it for the long haul. And so, I guess, am I.

Rules for Reverends

Jeremy Fletcher

Illustrated by Dave Walker

These 'rules' are not serious, really. Except the ones that are.

Clergy inhabit a fantastic, pressurised, privileged, frustrating and humbling role. They get to join in the highest and lowest points of people's lives, often on the same day. They have experiences. If they are very skilled they learn from them as well as laugh about them.

This book is for clergy like me, and anyone who does anything like the job of a parish priest. You might just recognise a few things, and you'll probably be able to think of some more. And it's for everyone we work with, minister among, share with, pray for and meet with. Normal people. If you're not quite sure what your ministers do all day, what they think about things, why they wear strange clothes, or what they really want to do with their congregation at the end of a busy Sunday, then *Rules for Reverends* will give you a clue.

ISBN 978 1 84101 657 3   £6.99
Available from your local Christian bookshop or direct from BRF:
please visit www.brfonline.org.uk

Travellers of the Heart

Exploring new pathways on our spiritual journey

Michael Mitton

In this book, one of the UK's leading authors on Christian spirituality and personal renewal shares his own faith journey, in the context of exploring some of the different spiritual traditions that have influenced Christian witness over the past 40 or so years.

Michael Mitton explores how encompassing the breadth of Christian spirituality, from Charismatic to Catholic, via Celtic, can not only enrich our faith but strengthen the mission of the church: 'I have chosen to start with my own experience, not because I am any kind of expert but because the best tutors to me over the years have been those prepared to share with me their stories, their ups and downs of life, their struggles and discoveries. Often their experiences have been very different from my own, but as I listen to them, they help me reflect on what is taking place in me.'

ISBN 978 0 85746 221 3   £7.99

Available from your local Christian bookshop or direct from BRF: please visit www.brfonline.org.uk

Enjoyed

this book?

Write a review–we'd love to hear what you think.
Email: reviews@brf.org.uk

Keep up to date–receive details of our new books as they happen.
Sign up for email news and select your interest groups at:
www.brfonline.org.uk/findoutmore/

Follow us on Twitter @brfonline

By post–to receive new title information by post (UK only), complete
the form below and post to: BRF Mailing Lists, 15 The Chambers, Vineyard,
Abingdon, Oxfordshire, OX14 3FE

Your Details
Name _____
Address_____
_____
Town/City _____ Post Code _____
Email_____

Your Interest Groups (*Please tick as appropriate)

- ☐ Advent/Lent
- ☐ Bible Reading & Study
- ☐ Children's Books
- ☐ Discipleship
- ☐ Leadership

- ☐ Messy Church
- ☐ Pastoral
- ☐ Prayer & Spirituality
- ☐ Resources for Children's Church
- ☐ Resources for Schools

Support your local bookshop
Ask about their new title information schemes.